Young Misery

A child and family psychiatrist discusses child and youth depression—how to identify it, and how to cope.

A guide for parents and professionals

Dr. David Palframan

 Published by Creative Bound International Inc.
1-800-287-8610
www.creativebound.com

ISBN 978-1-894439-29-9
Printed and bound in Canada
Copyright © 2007 Dr. David Palframan

This book is not intended to replace appropriate diagnosis and/or treatment, when indicated, by a qualified medical professional or physician. Case studies are composites and not specific to any given person. Any names used as examples throughout this book have been changed to ensure the privacy of individuals and families.

Production by Creative Bound International Inc.
Managing editor Gail Baird
Creative director Wendelina O'Keefe
Text editor Ruth Bradley-St-Cyr
Cover photo Wendelina O'Keefe
Author photo Tony Cuillerier
Illustration, page 25, Alessandra Cuti

Library and Archives Canada Cataloguing in Publication

Palframan, David S.

    Young misery : A child and family psychiatrist discusses child and youth depression—how to identify it, and how to cope. A guide for parents and professionals / David Palframan.

Includes bibliographical references.

ISBN 978-1-894439-29-9

    1. Depression in children—Popular works. 2. Depression in adolescence—Popular works. I. Title.

RJ506.D4P34 2006   618.92'8527   C2006-904555-0

To all my feisty patients.

Contents

Introduction

The treatment of child and youth mental health problems has been notoriously difficult and complex. Although each individual family with such problems is consumed by their concerns, society at large often seems either indifferent or hostile. We shouldn't be. The second most common cause of death in adolescence is suicide. Only motor vehicle accidents kill more teenagers and some of *them* are suicides. These deaths, painfully tragic for families and friends, are a perversion of the natural cycle of life where parents die before their children. All of our wit, wisdom, and tenacity need to be trained on these complex situations. The causes are seldom simple, but the search for relief and therapy is one that is both rewarding and educative.

The use of antidepressants in children under the age of 18 has been called into question with recent news that they can increase suicidal behavior. This news, together with the understandable unease connected with the use of drugs that affect the developing brains of children and adolescents, has caused many families to wonder which treatments are safe.

Antidepressant treatment for adults entered the modern era in the 1950s with tricyclic drugs. They worked about two-thirds of the time. As some patients regained their energy, they became more suicidal since they had lots of energy and were still intensely depressed. These patients were carefully supervised until their mood rose to match their energy levels. The recent discovery that as many as ten percent of children treated with many antidepressants (the SSRIs—Selective Serotonin Re-uptake Inhibitors) may develop an agitation response leading to suicidal behavior might be a similar problem. Far fewer depressed patients are hospitalized now than were in the 1950s through 1970s. Hospitalized patients are routinely under supervision but all people on antidepressants need careful supervision, especially if they show agitation. The burden of such vigilance falls mostly on parents, who are encouraged to become aware of side effects and contact the prescribing doctor if they have concerns. Sometimes drug side effects make things worse, not better, and in those cases a new approach must be attempted. Avoiding all drug treatment for depressed young people would, however, deprive them of an important benefit.

That said, treatment for depression requires more than attempting to alter brain chemistry. Remarkable comfort and hope comes from psychotherapy. For one thing, it helps to feel understood. As well, it is vital to hear that depression may feel like it will last forever, but it doesn't. Providing information in a hopeful context, supporting the depressed person, and helping them to discover their own techniques—first to live with and then to defeat the disease—are all vital aspects of treatment. The best results come from a combination of drug treatment and psychotherapy.

This book is a call to arms about child and youth depression.

There will never be enough child psychiatrists or other related specialists to treat all of its victims. Parents, teachers, family doctors, grandparents, and all of us who relate closely to children need to be more aware of depression in children and families. Then, once educated about it, we need to detect the condition quickly, talk about the problems and organize the best possible treatment and support.

• 1 •

The Symptoms of Depression in Children

Until recently, depression seemed to be either a normal reaction to sad or tragic personal misfortune or a state of mind that made some people miserable for no apparent reason. Were these people weak-willed or deliberately seeking attention? The reputation of depression was pretty bad and definitely associated with guilt and loss. No one thought that children could develop depression, except as a reaction to bad news. The feelings of children and teenagers appear to be a clear reflection of their environments. Child + ice-cream = grin. Fourteen-year-old girl + telephone + chatty friend = popularity and happiness. This view of children's emotions is wishful thinking. From fussy babies to gloomy adolescents, it is clear that individual variation in reaction to life's circumstances is extremely varied. As with adults, some children worry more, feel loss more keenly, and move unthinkingly from anxiety to anger.

Our present knowledge of depression has made it clear that the brain is distinctly changed during depression. The chemicals that speed the transmission of impulses from one nerve cell to another are not functioning properly. Various sorts of "brain-mapping" techniques reveal that serotonin and noradrenaline, two of the dozens of chemical neurotransmitters, or messengers, are deficient in the brains of depressed people. This evidence has caused depression to be reclassified both medically and in popular usage from a weak and unhappy personality to a disorder of the brain.

Is depression a disease, a disorder, or a condition of normal life? It's a matter of how intense and prolonged the low mood is. It also depends on whether the low mood is accompanied by serious anxiety, intense anger, sleeplessness, or sleep that leaves you still tired. Think of depression as a condition into which people slide, where self-confidence is reduced and life seems much less pleasurable. Without pleasure all that is left in life is the annoying worrisome and sad bits. Think of the tide going out: ripples of water recede, leaving damp rocks, slime, and junk.

Quite naturally a depressed child will struggle very hard to break free from the sticky grip of a depression. Some will seek pleasurable escapes, in the belief that pleasure is the antidote to depression. Pleasure, however, is momentary and not at all the same as happiness. Happiness is a spontaneous and pervasive state of mind that expresses delight in existence. Depressed people just can't get there.

Teenagers might find relief in angry attacks against parents or teachers, seeking pleasure from being rebellious. They might seek relief from drugs and alcohol, reckless driving, or the thrills of stealing, fighting, or careless sex. A totally reckless pursuit of pleasure might be a tip-off to an underlying depression.

• • •

Sadness is a necessary aspect of any observant person's life. However, if sadness is prolonged and intense beyond the nature of the circumstances, then the reasons for low mood might be sought within rather than without. Also, depression is both more and less than sadness. Children find that previous pleasures no longer give delight, so life is boring and without fun. Ordinary irritations become impossibly enraging frustrations. Depressed people feel that others probably don't like them, since their own sense of self-worth has fallen.

The results, in older children, are teenagers with high anxiety, poor concentration, low mood, and irritability. They may seek a lower-achieving and more destructive type of friend and they may be so uncaring of their future that addictive or delinquent thrill-seeking gives temporary relief from their misery.

Younger children who are depressed have a limited ability to express their mood in words. They, too, tend to be irritable and sad. They do worse in school and worry more about it. Mostly, they just seem to have lost their sparkle or their ability to have fun. Depression causes a reduction in the child's capacity to experience pleasure. When pleasure is drained out of life, what's left? Boredom, annoyance at minor disappointments, frustrations everywhere that are unrelieved by hope, and feelings that, since everyone else seems happy, "there must be something wrong with me" or "maybe I don't deserve good things."

Younger children and teenagers may be more restless or more slowed down, sleep more or sleep less, but whatever the changes are, they are not themselves and they aren't comfortable and happy.

As you can see, ordinary sadness looks and feels a lot like depression. However, sad people recognize what is making them sad and they can react positively to happy circumstances—a good joke, the company of cheerful people. Depressed people claim an inability to respond to the joys in life, and they tend to feel this is because of flaws within themselves. They start to ruminate about what failures they are and how awful life is. They begin to feel that life will never get better for them. The next step might be to feel suicidal.

For some people, their depression feels like a black hole without any escape. Children and adults alike may feel that their lives have always been sad and unfair. A list of the official symptoms of depression as described in the diagnostic manual of the American Psychiatric Association (APA) gives a sense of the heavy burden depressed people carry. You can check this symptom list at the end of the chapter.

Case History: Donny

Donny, age five, came to see me with his worried mom. She said he wasn't sleeping at night and he just wasn't himself. He cried easily, upset by small disappointments that didn't used to bother him. For example, his mom had served stew for supper instead of spaghetti. Donny had looked at his plate and started to cry. Later that night, he crept into bed with his mom and said he was scared. His kindergarten teacher said he looked sad and she remembered that he had been a cheery little guy only three months ago. He was refusing to join in group activities and he had quarreled with a friend.

Donny's parents were getting along well and there were no special stresses in the family. His mom had been depressed for several months three years ago and she had recovered on antidepressants. His dad was very kind and attentive to Donny and he said that he had been a lot like Donny when he was a boy—worried about every little thing, and often tearful.

I asked Donny about his life and he said it wasn't so good. He said he worried that the dog would get hit by a car and that bad men would come at night and hurt him or his parents. Donny didn't want to go to a birthday party scheduled for the next weekend. He just didn't feel like it.

When I saw Donny and his parents, there were several clues I used to decide what to do. Donny's mood was low, he worried non-stop and he had lost his capacity to enjoy life. The family history suggested both parents might well have had a susceptibility to depression and his mom had successfully used antidepressants. In the absence of other reasons for Donny's unhappiness, it seemed sensible to try an antidepressant. The newer antidepressants have fewer annoying side effects, such as dizziness, dry mouth, and constipation, than those developed forty years ago. No antidepressants are habit-forming. Donny took a pill every morning after breakfast and his parents called in a week to say that he seemed brighter, but his stomach hurt. I switched to another antidepressant, made sure he was taking it after breakfast, and a week later, Donny was sleeping through the night, in his own bed. Recovery was marked by better sleep, less worrying, a brighter mood, and a return to playing outside with his friends. He didn't miss the next birthday party.

Several years later, Donny still has periods of low confidence and high anxiety, but he is progressing well at school, and he has never been as extremely miserable as he was when I first saw him. He uses the same antidepressant, but at a maintenance dosage that is half the original dosage.

How Common Is Child and Youth Depression?

Surveys of adults show that almost one person in five will experience a depression at some time. This makes depression very common compared to other diseases, such as diabetes or arthritis. Many people suffer through their depressions without special treatment and most depressions will go away on their own. Unfortunately, depression can last from six weeks to many years. Waiting for it to go away is not a very attractive prospect. Moreover, depression can be fatal.

Suicide is very closely correlated with a depressive illness, and represents the death rate from this illness. Children under 13 appear to count on their parents for support. They may talk about life being very unhappy, or even wishing they were dead, but completing suicide seems to require the independence and the intense loneliness and aggression of a post-pubertal age.

The Burden of Suffering

Depressed adults, once recovered, speak eloquently of what Winston Churchill called "the black dog" of depression. Children and youth may lack the self-awareness to explain the pain of low self-esteem, guilt, sleeplessness, and inability to concentrate. They undoubtedly feel that "life sucks" and we watch them fail at school, complain bitterly about the smallest frustrations, and generally act and feel quite miserable. Because smaller children haven't yet developed much of an emotional language, they can't express these symptoms very directly. Their parents may experience some of the burden of this disorder in trying to cope with intense outbursts of rage. Tantrums, fighting, inability to pitch in with household chores—these expressions of unhappiness can make life with a depressed child most unpleasant. Parents may squabble about how to manage their cheerless and constantly complaining kid. Meanwhile at school, academic performance starts to slide and the child may show aggression and anxiety. The authorities often react with some concern, then some impatience at the aggression, or even with anger when the child doesn't "snap out of it."

Gender Differences in Depression

A gross generalization of the difference between the sexes would be to say that boys get mad and girls get sad. The differences noted between boys and girls in how they express feelings, begin with the striking yet commonplace fact that little boys are far more aggressive than little girls. They hit and punch and bite more, yank toys away from others, push in line-ups at recess, play war games, and fight.

Girls are more muted in their response to frustrations. They seek out close friendships, are more hesitant to be openly competitive, and look to adults to solve disputes. Indeed, girls often seem more socially advanced than boys, a reflection of a more rapid maturation of the female brain.

One advantage that the boys have is their ability to express rage or to externalize the conflict. The fault or the blame lies with someone else who is promptly attacked—a savage but briefly satisfying response. Little girls tend to hesitate or even to ruminate and are prone to more self-blame. More girls are depressed than are boys. More boys have aggressive conduct disorders than do girls.

By adolescence the results of these gender differences begin to become apparent. The males who become depressed experience a more deadly form of the illness since the misery of depression is combined with a habit or an expected gender role of violent behavior. Young males use much more violent means of expressing their low mood. Their self-destructive or reckless behavior is more intense. They drive faster, wreck their cars more often, drink more, and fight more. When they are almost crushed by their low mood, they seek out more lethal means of attempting suicide, such as hanging, shooting, and car crashes.

Young women are more likely to have previously expressed their unhappiness to others. They are more likely to have formed a support network to which they appeal when they feel miserable. Boys talk sports and punch each other on the shoulder, while girls share feelings. Girls try suicide more often, using overdoses or wrist-cutting, and leaving notes and signs in obvious places, hoping the clues will be read by concerned parents and friends. As a result, fewer girls die by suicide and more get help. Boys feel more isolated and may actually be more isolated by the restrictions of their gender role. In short, girls get sad, boys get mad.

What we see in children becomes even clearer in adults, where more women than men ask for help for their low mood, ask for help earlier, and use non-lethal methods for attempting suicide. The pattern, then, is for females to suffer openly from depression more often than males, and for a longer period. When males get depressed, the situation is usually more acute and more often lethal. Interestingly enough, this disease pattern difference between females and males is reflected in many other areas of medicine, in that women tend to have more chronic, remitting-relapsing, non-fatal disorders and men have more acute, fatal disorders.

What use can we make of these generalizations? The most obvious response has been to appeal to males to speak up about their feelings so that early intervention and better support can be offered. Also, society clearly deplores the extremes of male violence and suggests that a testosterone-driven life is as dangerous as a Ferrari without brakes. The results of the efforts to alter male "weaknesses" are not yet clear, but it would seem wise to channel aggression into socialized directions. Depending on a boy's talents and interests, he might do well in team or individual sports. Many boys enjoy the intensity and sheer fun of music or "improv" comedy. The aggression won't go away but it can be focused constructively. Teams are better than gangs; great causes are superior to petty revenge. Such matters run very deeply in a society and our success in dealing with them is a reflection of our maturity as a civilized people.

Key Points

From fussy babies to gloomy adolescents, it is clear to experienced parents and doctors that some children are very different from the average in how they react to life's challenges. Some children worry more, feel disappointment and frustration more keenly, and move unthinkingly from anxiety to anger. Many of these children go on to develop depression or related disorders.

This brief overview shows how depression is experienced by young people and how it changes their behavior. Without understanding the process beneath their behavior, it is only natural to condemn the behavior, pass it off as laziness or try to punish the kid into being better. When we see the bigger picture, we can also begin to make clear plans to effect improvement. Children and adults can begin to work together instead of co-existing in a soup of worry and anger.

Common symptoms of depression include:
- reduced ability to experience pleasure
- irritability
- insomnia
- low energy
- low self-esteem

Boys and girls show depression differently:
- boys are more aggressive
- boys have a hard time sharing feelings
- girls ask for help more readily
- girls get sad; boys get mad

**Official symptoms of depression from
the American Psychiatric Association:**

At least four of the following symptoms have each been present nearly every day for a period of at least two weeks (in children under six, at least three of the first four):

1. Poor appetite or significant weight loss (when not dieting) or increased appetite or significant weight gain (in children under six, consider failure to make expected weight gains)

2. Insomnia or hypersomnia (too much sleep without feeling restless)

3. Psychomotor agitation or retardation (but not merely subjective feelings of restlessness or being slowed down); (in children under six, reduced activity)

4. Loss of interest or pleasure in usual activities, or decrease in sexual drive not limited to a period when delusional or hallucinating (in children under six, signs of apathy)

5. Loss of energy; fatigue

6. Feelings of worthlessness, self-reproach, or excessive or inappropriate guilt (either may be delusional)

7. Complaints or evidence of diminished ability to think or concentrate, such as slowed thinking, or indecisiveness not associated with marked loosening of associations or incoherence

8. Recurrent thoughts of death, suicidal ideation, wishes to be dead, or suicide attempt

• 2 •

Causes of Depression

Even though the condition of depression is likely associated with an imbalance in brain neurotransmitters such as serotonin, noradrenaline, and norepinephrine, there are many circumstances that may combine to produce this chemical situation. How we feel about ourselves and our lives clearly has an effect on our bodies, as anyone who has blushed in embarrassment or vomited in nervousness knows. This chapter will discuss how some of life's events can gang up on a young person and sometimes push them into a depression. Some people seem almost invulnerable to depression no matter how tough their lives get. Still others appear to become depressed out of the blue, without any reasonable evidence of pressures or troubles from outside. Falling into a depression occurs because of some combination of personal intrinsic factors, together with an accumulation of troubles in life.

Brain Chemistry

The diagram below attempts to show how antidepressants are designed to reverse the chemical problem in the depressed person's brain. Nerve fibers connect and pass on electrical impulses using a device called the synapse. This is a space that acts as a switch to either block or transmit nerve signals. If too many switches block the impulse, brain activity is reduced. Depression is associated with a reduction in brain activity in the frontal lobe, behind the forehead. Not all activity is reduced, but mainly the activity governed by the neurotransmitter chemicals noradrenaline and serotonin. Scientists attempt to overcome this reduced activity by increasing the amounts of these chemicals. Unfortunately we can't just eat more of the stuff, since neurotransmitters are simple

What happens with nerve cells when antidepressants are used

A. Site of blockade of neurotransmitter re-uptake
B. Vesicle containing neurotransmitter such as serotonin or noradrenalin
C. Nerve impulse
D. Continuation of nerve impulse

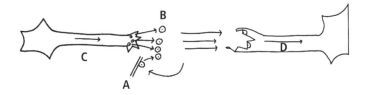

Actions which increase activity of neurotransmitters

chemicals and easily broken down in the stomach or in the blood. A person can get brief relief from natural endorphins by exercising intensely for twenty minutes or so. This produces a natural "high." Unfortunately, depressed people seldom feel much like exercising and the relief is brief. Regular exercise definitely helps keep depression away once the low mood has been partly improved.

The drugs that work against depression can block serotonin re-uptake or increase the amount available by other means. The other two techniques (as illustrated in the diagram on page 25) for increasing neurotransmitters work about 70 percent of the time to give temporary relief; however, all alone, they won't be enough to treat a serious depression. Increasing dosages of the pills, or using a combination of pills, will help a few more people.

People should definitely do positive activities that help improve their mood, as well as taking medication. The important role of psychotherapy is dealt with in a later chapter and is entirely compatible with medication, music and exercise.

There are some helpful indicators of when antidepressant drugs will work. They are more likely to be effective if one or more close family members are or have been depressed and have gotten better on antidepressants. Having depression with or without anxiety in close family members suggests that antidepressants may work. Sleep problems, lack of energy, and a general reduction in the ability to enjoy activities the individual used to like, suggest that the depression has a basis in altered brain activity and is not a reaction to a sad environment.

Antidepressant medications work gradually, and can take up to six weeks to begin reducing the symptoms. When things are going better, these medications should be used for four to six months. If all is well, a gradual doctor-supervised dose reduction is a good idea. Sometimes there can be temporary nervousness and unease for three or four days. Dose reduction needs to be gradual. If symptoms return, the medication should be restarted.

About two in three people will get better due in part to antidepressants. Some will need to try a different one, due to uncomfortable side effects. Doctors need to be told if the medicine isn't working. The dose may need to go up. There are ten or more antidepressants, and some can be used in combination. The doctor and the family need to work together, persistently, to find the right antidepressant at the right dosage, with minimal side effects.

Antidepressants, however, are only part of the answer to treatment. They take a long time to take effect—up to six weeks. They often have side effects such as headaches, nausea, excess sweating, reduction of sex drive, or agitation. A depressed person may need to try two, three, or four different medicines before finding the right pill or combination of pills. And what about the group of people who get no help or only partial help from these medicines?

Doctors know that the pills alone are not enough. They often help tremendously but other forms of treatment must also be used. Informed, personal support through psychotherapy helps. Reducing personal stress helps. Improving family life, taking regular exercise, discarding addictions, and learning to be an assertive and effective problem solver—all of these concepts are parts of the solution. A pill is very seldom a magic bullet.

Genetics, Pre-disposing Disorders, and Life Events

Although we readily sense that hair colour, facial features, and even baldness are associated with inheritance, people find it more difficult to accept that many psychiatric disorders are partly determined by genetic inheritance. The resistance to a genetic explanation is due partly to a sense of shame, of coming from a family with a taint or flaw. Also, there is already a prejudice against people with psychiatric problems and it seems unfair to point fingers at people and say they have a genetic flaw. The evidence, however, is pretty strong. Population studies show that many disease states, including depression, cluster in families.

Scientists have studied the genetics of depression, and found a distinct inherited pattern in some situations. Most obviously, if an identical twin becomes depressed then the other twin has about an 80 percent probability of being depressed at the same time, even if the twins were separated at birth and raised in different families. The more close relatives a person has with depression, the more likely it is that this person will become depressed. This is true for children and teenagers as well as for adults.

Molecular studies of the genetic material (DNA) from people with depression are beginning to show specific changes in the code, much in the way that similar studies have shown changes in the genetic code of people with cystic fibrosis, some types of diabetes, and some types of hypertension. The brain, after all, is an organ, a piece of specialized material, and some errors in its construction can occur if the plans are slightly in error. As is the case with many genetically related disorders, we don't know precisely which chromosomal material is responsible for the genetic vulnerability for depression and most of the evidence is statistical rather than biochemical.

While genetic vulnerability is one of the built-in aspects of depression, DNA alone does not usually cause depression. Most often it is miserable life events that trigger depression. A large proportion of depressed people are perfectionistic and hard to please. Even as children, they fear failure, don't give themselves credit for normal success, and fuss and worry over minor problems. Such a personality, called obsessive-compulsive, is likely inborn and it is easy to see how such a child has difficulty having fun and being tolerant of life's imperfections.

The best description of the life events that seem to push people towards depression comes from an examination of the circumstances of suicidal people—a topic dealt with in more detail in chapter five. Depressed people often have had more than their fair share of life events that have deprived them of the capacity to enjoy life. As children, many were so neglected or abused that they developed attachment disorders, best understood as an inability and lack of desire to love others, because early life showed them that their parents were unreliable and unloving. The inability to create and sustain a mutually satisfying love relationship with friends, parents, or romantic partners makes it extra hard to get through life's difficult times.

Anxiety also runs in families, and is likely part of the built-in "hard wiring" of depression. These are people who have the dubious gift of worrying—people who are talented in noticing what has gone wrong and what *might* go wrong. Their overall alertness to problems is often combined with acute attacks of intense anxiety, where they experience nervous sweating, rapid heartbeat, a strong sense of panicky doom, and a feeling of suffocation. A more focused form of acute anxiety is phobic disorder, where a person has a specific trigger (heights, insects, crowds) that precedes an acute anxiety attack. Eating disorders, such as anorexia nervosa, involve a fear of getting fat and these ailments are related statistically and genetically to depression and anxiety states.

Somewhere in between the built-in and the circumstances-of-life type of factors is the concept of "learned helplessness." This attitude, if portrayed by someone in the family, suggests that passively accepting problems without displaying any fighting spirit is a reasonable and inevitable way to live. Such people fail to use and fail to teach their children necessary coping, struggling, and problem-solving skills. Their children learn by example that when the going gets tough, you sink. The devoutly helpless also blame others for their problems and have little skill in solving their own problems.

Now that a few of the remote (genetic) and predisposing (anxiety states, phobias, eating disorders, obsessive-compulsive disorders) factors contributing to depression are in place, it takes little imagination to set up a scenario where something triggers a depression in such a person. Freud summed it up well by explaining that when a person suffers a loss of something or someone important, and then feels angry and guilty about the loss, depression often follows. In children, common losses are the loss of friends who move away, moving away yourself and losing your friends, losing a parent due to separation or divorce, and losing your health due to a disease or disability. The downward spiral in mood can then trigger lower school marks, less interest in friends who then drop the child, and irritability, which further alienates everyone.

In teenagers, all of the unhappy losses already mentioned for younger children may apply but there are a few additional troubles. Teenagers are much more sensitive about their physical appearance than are younger children. Acne, obesity, delayed puberty, or any significant deviation from what is considered to be the ideal can become the focus of considerable concern or even despair. Teenage girls of a certain perfectionistic personality type are vulnerable to anorexia, a disorder closely related to society's pressure to be slim and closely related to depression. They seek a "perfect," impossibly slim body. This relationship between depression and anorexia will be explored further in chapter three.

Teenage boys, and a growing number of teenage girls, often try to cope with the extra irritability and aggression of puberty by using drugs and alcohol to conform, to enjoy risk-taking and to "chill out." Such drug taking is definitely associated with lowering self-esteem. It also reduces judgment, releases aggression, and is likely to involve the drinker or drug user in behavior about which they will feel genuine shame and sadness. The most dangerous drug is alcohol since it can cause depression of mood as well as addiction.

Another chemical difference after puberty is the ability to fall in love. No one really knows if love is chemical, but the phenomenon doesn't happen until after puberty, so maybe a certain brain chemical arrangement in conjunction with sex hormones is required. In any case, to fall in love is to be at risk of being rejected. Rejection in love is a powerful push towards depression in teenagers. Not only is the pain intense, but the sense of being inadequate is particularly poignant. Being dumped romantically is quite commonly mentioned in suicide notes, and it may provide just enough extra misery to cause a depression in a vulnerable person. The practice of a psychological autopsy after a teenager has died by suicide very commonly reveals a broken romance just prior to the death.

The Special Pain of Separation and Divorce

Marriage was a relatively stable if not always happy arrangement up until the 1960s. In response to a public demand for more personal freedom, divorce laws were loosened. Now about 45 percent of new marriages will not last a lifetime. Younger children tend to feel guilty, confused, angry, and scared when a parent leaves. Finances are less stable, and one or both parents may be unhappy and/or preoccupied. When parents share physical custody of their children following a separation or divorce, children commonly will be called upon to move back and forth between two homes, two bedrooms, two neighborhoods… If one or both parents remarry or create a blended family with a new partner, an often happy and helpful situation for the adults involved can present a new set of problems for the children. Where do their loyalties lie? Why must they share their parent and their home with another adult and with his or her children? Will there be room for the child in the new relationship(s)? Clearly these are practical issues that cause great worry in children.

Ongoing anger between the parents is particularly unwelcome to the children, who don't like to take sides and who usually wish to preserve a loving relationship with both parents. The scenario of pre-separation conflict, followed by the departure of a parent, and then the uncertainty of new arrangements can often precipitate a state of depression. Children who have lost a parent by death (except suicide) actually do better than children whose parents leave by choice. After their parents have split up, children gradually learn the underlying causes for the end of the marriage and, from their perspective, parents should really be ashamed of themselves. They tell their kids to get along when they squabble, while permitting themselves to change partners due to incompatibility. We hate it when our children lie or are unreliable, yet we excuse a growing frequency of infidelity as being part of human nature.

Children are often furious after a marital split but directing this anger at parents can be dangerous. First, the parent can get angry right back and second, the children feel very insecure about their place in their parents' hearts. After all, if love between parents can erode and disappear, what about the parents' love for a child? Instead, anger is often expressed indirectly: more aggression by boys and more antisocial behavior in both boys and girls. Much of this plays out at school rather than at home.

Long-term studies of the effects of separation and divorce on children have tracked people into their thirties. Although most are no longer preoccupied by their parents' separation, most also complain that the event was very painful and had long-lasting effects. These children, when grown, have a higher than average divorce rate and rate of depression.

Adult studies of the reasons for marital conflict often show that if a spouse is depressed, he or she becomes critical of the partner and is generally dissatisfied with life. That, after all, is what defines depression—an inability to experience pleasure. In an effort to be happier, the depressed spouse may well seek and find a new partner, creating a situation of exciting novelty and temporary but intense pleasure. This new drama, together with the critical view of their partner, is often enough to kill off the marriage. After a few years, the new partner, who has usually failed to "cure" the depression, may not look so great. Depressed parents can stress and even wreck marriages and this causes terrible suffering for their children. Along with a growing realization that children need their parents' marriages to remain healthy, we need to foster awareness that adultery doesn't fix depression. See a therapist. Renovate yourself. Don't rush to replace your spouse.

Teenagers often profess indifference about their parents'

marital problems, but underneath this facade lurk serious conflicts, anger, guilt, and anxiety. Teenagers worry about the family's finances, they resent having to move, and they have anger and contempt for the mess their parents have made of things. They would prefer to take for granted the boring stability of their parents, and being exposed to the dramatic and messy spectacle of parental separation prevents them from moving ahead with their own development. Home base is now insecure. Do you forsake your family and move out early? Do you stay home to comfort mom or dad? Do you become cynical about romantic love? Do you seek a dependable romantic partner to provide security for your life? No wonder many teenagers are sidetracked by parents' separation and divorce and begin to underachieve, act delinquent, or make very poor choices. They say they don't care about their parents' marriage, but its healthy existence is a prerequisite for a healthy passage through adolescence.

Nothing I have mentioned about the effects of separation and divorce on children is a specific cause of depression, but all of the potential reactions reveal a weakening of security, a reduction in family happiness, and a questioning of how well life will turn out for them.

Case History: Jason

When I first met Jason, the prospects for his improvement were dim. He was in the eighth grade and his mom told me that his usual recess consisted of his watching the other guys throw a football and refusing to let him get involved. Jason was an "okay" athlete, but he was in a learning disabilities class and under the iron rules of Grade Eight boys, he was a leper. His dad had recently moved back home, having lived in an apartment for eight months following a series of affairs. The dad seemed sincere in his desire to make his marriage work better. Jason's mother was cautious, bitter, and reluctant to share her life again now that she had learned how to run things on her own as a single parent.

I admired Jason's dad's persistence. He certainly had to eat large helpings of humble pie, served by both his kids and his wife. He repeatedly acknowledged his responsibility for the affairs, but he added an explanation: He had been depressed and angry for years. He hated his background, which featured a demanding and selfish mother who was notorious in the family for having bitten her husband because he got lost driving her home from a shopping trip. Jason's grandfather had Alzheimer's disease and was soon hospitalized, but the grandmother flew into a frenzy at the slightest personal frustration. Jason's dad said that at work, he was seen as a cheerful, flirtatious guy, whom the men didn't take very seriously. The women sensed his anxious sadness and comforted him. Their arms and bodies only made life more complicated and unbearable. His doctor helped him get some perspective and he started a course of antidepressant medication. Even his wife said that she could only stand him when he was on his pills. "He used to scream at me when he did the bills. Everything was out of control and we were always wrecking his life. It was such a relief when he left. Do I want him back? Not really, but…" The couple worked hard on their relationship, encouraged by his buoyant mood and her newly acquired personal confidence.

Jason was delighted and even moved by his parents' reconciliation. He was sent to a special school where he learned how to deal with his dyslexia. When he was 17 years of age, he suffered a serious depression. He was way ahead of me, thanks to the sensitive and alert actions of his parents and the openness in the family about depression. He recovered quickly on medication and, like his dad, he takes a maintenance dose of an antidepressant. Perhaps of equal importance, he knows and respects himself, flaws and qualities alike.

I've kept in touch with Jason, who is now in his early twenties. He works in a restaurant and plays drums in a band. His parents are together and they are proud that their son has a happier life. He is proud that they decided to change, work out their problems, and stay married.

Jason wouldn't be the courageous and healthy man he is today if his parents hadn't reconciled. He told me about some teachers who had been supportive to him, and their remarks and helpful attitude probably helped him through many tough times. Teachers are often part of a vulnerable child's "compensation package." Depressions in this family didn't quite sink his ship.

Key Points

Depression cannot usually be pinpointed to one cause but rather a combination of genetic predisposition and other factors, including traumatic life events:

- We tend to inherit a vulnerability to depression—it runs in families

- People who have anxiety attacks or phobias are more vulnerable to depression

- People who are obsessive-compulsive (very picky, rigid, very neat, controlling, guilt-ridden) are more vulnerable to depression

- People with eating disorders such as anorexia nervosa and bulimia are more vulnerable to depression

- "Learned helplessness" contributes to depression

- Divorce and separation contribute to depression in children

- Some acts of delinquency are due to low self-esteem and depression

• 3 •

Disorders That Accompany Depression

The term co-morbidities refers to conditions that appear quite commonly in conjunction with depression. Either the depression causes these other problems to develop, as with some forms of delinquency, or the co-morbid condition worsens and depression emerges. Another possibility is that different psychiatric disorders, which were formerly considered to be quite distinct, are caused by the same changes in brain chemistry. The disease of depression or the disease of obsessive-compulsive disorder differ in presentation but not cause, just as a bacterial infection in the lung is called pneumonia and an infection in the tonsils is called tonsillitis. A core set of causes involving neurotransmitters in different areas of the brain may explain why diseases group together in the same child.

Triple Trouble

Anxiety, obsessive-compulsive disorders, and phobias were once thought to be adult neuroses or habits of mind developed to deal with inner conflicts. At present, doctors view these disorders as being built in to the individual's brain through their neurotransmitter systems.

Anxiety

Anxiety attacks cripple people when they are overwhelmed by a sense of dread. The heart rate goes up, they can't seem to get enough air, their palms sweat, and they have to be with someone they know in safe, familiar surroundings. As adults, they may feel they're having a heart attack. The chemistry that underlies anxiety attacks is largely corrected by antidepressant drugs that restore the correct balance between and amongst serotonin, noradrenaline, and the many other small molecules that preside over nerve conduction in the brain. Children as young as three or four years can have anxiety episodes. They can't go to parties unless mom is there too. They may not be able to attend school. They couldn't begin to consider going to an overnight camp when they are nine or ten years old.

Obsessive-Compulsive Disorder

Obsessive-compulsive disorder refers to a range of symptom intensity. Some people have an overall personality that features perfectionism and a preoccupation with trivial details or a controlling and bossy attitude, an over-conscientious approach to work and duty, and problems making decisions because it's hard to risk being wrong. Such people are likely born that way. There is certainly a strong genetic line of evidence suggesting that this is inherited. If the person (young or old) has inherited a lot of these traits (high "penetrance" of the genetic material) then they may develop obsessions and compulsions. Obsessions are repeated ideas and thoughts that are unwelcome. Commonly they are worried about horrible tragedies. A little girl might think constantly about getting sick and vomiting, or about her parents dying in a car crash. Having such obsessive thoughts makes it hard to concentrate on school work or even to relax and have fun.

Compulsions are behaviors that obsessive people are pushed to do. These acts, such as hand-washing or checking to see if the door is locked or the stove is off, appear to be logical but they are performed to excess. The sufferer can try to not perform the compulsion, but this causes such great anxiety that it's easier to just get out of bed and check the doors and windows (for the fifth time).

Children with obsessive-compulsive disorder can be hard to cope with. On the positive side, they are usually obedient, intelligent, and hard-working. When their disorder slides into a depression, things are not so positive. Their obsessive-compulsive symptoms worsen and the usual symptoms of depression are piled on top.

Phobias

Phobias are apparently unreasonable fears of certain situations. Players of word games may enjoy the names of specific phobias—agoraphobia (fear of open spaces), claustrophobia (fear of closed spaces), triskaidekaphobia (fear of the number thirteen), and so on. Phobias are no joke. They are highly intense, and require the person to avoid any situation where the feared situation might occur. Life then has to be restricted accordingly. Unfortunately, phobic people usually have a lot of general anxiety about life and a lot of them are somewhat obsessive-compulsive. They, too, are more than usually vulnerable to depression and when depression hits these people, their ability to function is very, very damaged. As children, they can't attend school without being terribly anxious, even though they may be good students. They may need to sleep in their parents' bed, though formerly they were comfortable in their own rooms. Their families are forced to adopt elaborate schemes to make sure that the phobic child is never alone. No amount of reassurance is enough. And, with depression, the fun goes out of life, the anxieties get worse, the poor kid can't sleep, and even suicide seems better than this kind of torment.

Case History: Joanne

I first met Joanne when she was five years old. It was February and this child, who formerly loved her kindergarten, was so anxious about school that she refused to go. She would lie on the floor, kicking, screaming, and crying. She clung like a limpet to her mom rather than join her chums in the play group. Joanne had always been a very proper child, said her mom, a child who was neat, polite, and considerate. Her parents readily tolerated her picky eating habits and her need to wear only those clothes that felt "right" against her skin. For example, Joanne wouldn't eat her food if the carrots were touching the potatoes, or if the gravy was not placed in its own isolated puddle. A new plate had to be prepared. One of her new dresses had an elasticized waist that bunched the fabric at the small of her back so that when she sat down, it felt funny. She wore that dress only once.

Joanne wasn't spoiled. Her parents exercised reasonable discipline. Their home was orderly and had stable routines. When her quirks and her fussy perfectionism moved into terrible anxiety that something might go wrong if she went to school, her parents were very upset. Joanne developed trouble going to sleep at night unless mommy and daddy checked that the doors and windows were locked. Then she refused to go to school.

I met two very concerned parents and a distraught and very sad little girl. She cried during most of the interview. She said that she had no friends and she was afraid her parents were going to get sick and die or have a terrible accident. A check of the family history did not reveal any tragedies or problems about which Joanne might reasonably be worried. Joanne's mom had had a depression when she was about 18 years of age, and her dad said he understood his daughter's finicky habits. At work, he couldn't start his day unless all of his pencils were lined up in order of size at the right upper corner of his desk. Joanne's perfectionistic and anxious basic personality had, perhaps under a self-imposed pressure to succeed at school, propelled her into a full-blown depressive state. Happily, she recovered well on antidepressant medication and she was restored to her formerly finicky but charming and happy self.

Joanne's list of diagnoses includes anxiety, obsessive-compulsive traits, phobias, and depression. Instead of having four separate illnesses that just happen to be controlled by the same medicine, she probably has only one underlying disorder. A lot of diseases present with different symptoms at different times but with only one underlying cause.

Attention-Deficit Hyperactivity Disorder (ADHD)

Charles Dickens wrote a brilliant description of a hyperactive child 140 years ago. "Peck's bad boy" was fidgety, argumentative, talkative, and couldn't pay attention to his lessons any longer than a butterfly could stay put on a single flower. Our best understanding of such children is that they are born with a lot of drive, more than average sensitivity to stress, low tolerance to frustration, and a huge need to be stimulated. These children, most of whom are boys, have a short attention span, are highly impulsive, and usually are very, very active. Their brains are driven faster than average, like a high-powered car with feeble brakes. Managing the situation requires an appreciation for their amazing energy and a calm and strong ability to set limits and establish routines. They learn best in small groups that present stimulation in a one-thing-at-a-time, short-lesson model. Sometimes, when high structure and predictable routines are not enough to keep them from climbing the curtains, they may benefit from minor stimulant medications such as methylphenidate (Ritalin) or dextroamphetamine (Dexedrine). These medicines are designed to restore balance in the neurotransmitter systems so that the child is less restless and less impulsive. They can be very helpful as learning tools but, of course, they don't replace the need for very careful parenting.

ADHD has a lot of advantages. Hyperactive people need less sleep, have more energy, are often excellent athletes (very quick reflexes), and love to take initiatives that might frighten more cautious people. There is, of course, a downside of ADHD. First, it has a genetic aspect and if a hyperactive little boy has a hyperactive parent, the necessary patience for managing a high maintenance child may not be there. Two hair-trigger tempers in the same family means trouble. Secondly, about 40 percent of people with ADHD are vulnerable to a depressive disorder. This depression is different from the low self-esteem that ADHD kids may develop due to being criticized all the time. What happens is a real clinical depression with pervasive sadness, irritability, and sleep disturbance. When life sucks for an ADHD child, their already intense nature, usually sunny and fun-seeking, becomes bitterly critical and sometimes violent. A few of them need to come off their medications, which sometimes contribute to the depression, and most of them will need antidepressant drug treatment.

As you can imagine, the stress on the family is huge. ADHD is a tough situation to manage and when depression is added, parents and teachers, brothers and sisters all need to be extra-patient and extra-determined to restore behavioral control and a better mood. The worst situations occur when the child begins to bully and hurt those around him. This might feed the child's sense of power and result in a kid who is compensating for a low mood by damaging the world and wrecking his own reputation and self-esteem.

The co-morbidity of ADHD and depression is both common and extra tough to manage. Almost half of the children with ADHD have trouble learning to read. Imagine the frustration of an impatient child who can't crack the code of written language despite good teaching and a normal intelligence. These children get letters out of order, write letters backwards (such as b for d) and can only read and write after years of tedious practice. Children will say that the letters they are looking at move around, even though they write all the letters in the word—for example, pasghetti for spaghetti. They don't automatically go from left to right and top to bottom. They may pay attention to the white spaces between words and lines just as much as they do to the letters. Careful psychological testing helps clarify the problem which affects both reading and spelling. This specific learning disability is called dyslexia and it is a most painful addition to the problems of children with ADHD.

Delinquency

Delinquency is a legal term, referring to illegal behavior such as shoplifting and vandalism. There are multiple causes of delinquent behavior, and amongst them is depression. If an adolescent is experiencing a depressed mood, the ability to concentrate at school is often reduced. Marks may suffer. The teenager may be unusually sensitive to criticism and become highly irritable. As self-esteem drops, the child may change life goals and decide that success is not likely so why not just give up? Escapes from the pain of depression may include drinking and drugs. These activities cost money and are usually pursued with like-minded, alienated peers. Illegal acts such as shoplifting or housebreaking may provide an escape from depression by the sheer thrill of defying authority.

Those depressed teenagers who use delinquency to cope with depression end up by expressing anger, devaluing themselves, and placing themselves at serious risk legally and socially. The kind of feedback they get from adults only confirms their worst fears—that they are losers who deserve a bad life. Such children are usually not the same as chronic conduct disordered children whose antisocial behavior often dates back many years. They are more likely to be unhappy about their delinquency than proud of it, and when their depression is addressed, they often eliminate the delinquency very quickly.

There is an additional, troubling form of delinquency associated with neglect. Chronic stealing, beginning in the pre-school years and perhaps including the hoarding of food, is often a tip-off to a child with an attachment disorder. Attachment disorder is caused by serious and prolonged neglect in the first twelve to twenty-four months of life. Babies who don't get much response from adults when they need something seem to make a kind of inner shift. They stop depending on caretakers and they become self-centered and self-seeking, as they age. They are forced by neglect to find food and playthings, and they partly give up on using relationships with others to meet their needs. Stealing by a child with attachment disorder has a different quality from that of most delinquent acts. Their behavior is relentlessly self-serving and their relationships are superficial. As they grow up, their anger and sadness, caused by having no reliable love relationships, causes great anguish.

Bipolar Disorder

Most depressions follow a course where mood slumps, then rises to near normal. About 15 percent are more complex, in that the sufferer experiences periods of excitement, restlessness, irritability, and accelerated thinking. This state of near-elation is called hypomania. At its most intense, people feel grandiose and their judgment socially, financially, and sexually is terrible. They don't need much sleep and their thoughts race. Hypomanic states result in dangerous behavior, since there is no way, short of hospitalization, to dissuade the sufferer from their impulses. By then, a great deal of damage may have occurred—money fraudulently obtained and spent, substances and people abused, family members embarrassed and disgusted.

People with bipolar disorder may have periods of intense delinquency, promiscuity, and substance abuse in their teens. Usually a family history reveals other relatives who had a similar pattern of behavior that, over time, settled into a more routinized series of depressions. Such people tend to be brighter than average and are often quite talented and charismatic. Treatment with mood-stabilizing drugs such as lithium carbonate or valproic acid allows them to use their talents without being interrupted by the dangerous raptures of hypomania or the hellishness of depression. Without treatment, people almost become addicted to the disorder, remembering their hypomania and hoping to outlast their depressions. Suicide rates are high in this population.

Mood instability is not unusual in children and in adolescents. When mood changes without any apparent environmental trigger, and the change is intense and bizarre, a bipolar disorder may be beginning. Sleeplessness, restlessness, grandiosity, rapid speech, and intense exhibitionism might sound like fun, but the results are usually awful, especially when the cycle shifts abruptly into depression. Rapid-cycling children, whose mood shifts several times in a single day, need to see a doctor fast.

Only the most dramatic childhood cases of bipolar disorder—with intense symptoms of rapid, joking speech, grandiose moods, pressured thinking, extreme sociability, and reckless judgment—will be diagnosed before puberty. Most people with bipolar disorder are in their twenties before the pattern of recurrent mood disorders of highs and lows becomes clear. Since a significant number of children with recurrent depressions will go on to develop a bipolar disorder, these children will need special scrutiny and follow-up. The underlying depressive disorder seems to continue, despite good treatment. Then there are more episodes of reckless behavior and wild mood swings. Discriminating between adolescent exuberance and genuine hypomanic surges can be diffi-cult. Using mood-stabilizing medications such as lithium carbon-ate and valproic acid can reduce the frequency and intensity of the mood swings, and can sometimes partially prevent the recurrence of depression. Treatment resistance in these young people is quite common since they enjoy the freedom from inhibition and the grandiosity connected to hypomania. Bipolar disorder is con-nected later in life to perhaps one-quarter of cases of childhood depression, and the management of this disorder is complicated by the extra dimensions of hypomania.

Schizophrenia

Schizophrenia is a group of disorders characterized chemically by an over-activity of the neurotransmitter dopamine. Unlike depres-sion, where the chemical problems appear to be mostly in the frontal part of the brain, the chemical disorder in schizophrenia is in the middle part of the inner core of the brain. At any rate, peo-ple with schizophrenia have a mixture of several of the following symptoms: auditory hallucinations (usually hearing voices), unre-sponsive or inappropriate expression of feelings, illogical and idio-syncratic thought patterns, inability to proceed from thought to action, and bizarre paranoid delusions. These disorders begin to appear in the mid- to late teens and a few teenagers with early schizophrenia may appear to be depressed. They withdraw from social activities and they appear to have no interest in former pleasures. They sense, vaguely, that life isn't what it should be, or was, and their overall activity and productivity decline. Over time, other more bizarre symptoms appear such as paranoid delusions, thought disorders, and hearing voices. Before these symptoms make a diagnosis of schizophrenia clear, efforts to treat depression have often begun and such treatment doesn't do any harm, but it doesn't do much good either.

Schizophrenia is not the only disease that can mimic clinical depression. It's much more common for people to feel clinically depressed just after the acute phase of several viral illnesses. Influenza virus and infectious mononucleosis are notorious for being associated with a depressive state that may last for a few months after the acute disorder has passed.

Self-Mutilation

The most primitive form of self-mutilation is seen during temper tantrums. An enraged and frustrated toddler will bang her head, kick her heels on the floor, or hold her breath. Putting the blackmailing "Mommy, you better do what I want" message to one side, such children find temporary relief from their frustrations by causing themselves pain. So intense are their feelings that they appear not to feel the pain very much. Later in life, during fits of anger, children will kick doors or punch walls hard enough to hurt themselves. Clearly, then, anger is a necessary component for self-harm. During depression, some older children, usually girls, will begin to deal with depression and anger by cutting themselves. The sites chosen are the forearms, thighs, calves and breasts. The cuts are not life-threatening, but they send a message of pain and anger. The girls say that the cutting precedes relief, temporarily, from the pains of depression and frustration. Often these girls are unhappy with their bodies and not very assertive in solving problems in relationships.

This cutting is different from a suicide attempt and indeed the girls report that self-mutilation averts suicidal impulses. The physical pain caused by slowly and delicately drawing a razor blade across the skin and dividing the top layers just enough to bleed seems to be minimal. Many self-mutilating girls clearly feel relief from depression and possibly the cutting causes a release of serotonin or certain encephalon chemicals in the brain. These substances, like the endorphins produced in a "runner's high," may well elicit a short-term, pleasurable feeling. A further "benefit" of self-mutilation is found in its guilt-reducing impact. Just as wearing a hair shirt, starving oneself or whipping oneself on the back with a knotted cord relieved the guilt of religious monks and hermits centuries ago, so self-mutilation may reduce the guilt and depression of some of today's guilt-ridden young people.

Cutting the skin can arrest an anxiety attack in the same way that stubbing your toe smartly against the furniture can divert your attention from any number of worries—at least briefly. Finally, where chronic anxiety and depression have numbed a person into barely feeling anything—a kind of defensive shell called depersonalization—self-mutilation reconnects the sufferer to reality.

Since it's clear that the symptom doesn't represent a threat to life, we should help the child to find another way to deal with guilt, depression, and anxiety. Effectively treating the underlying depression will end self-mutilation. Other less damaging outlets, such as intense exercise, can be suggested. Fundamentally, self-mutilation must be seen as an attempt to improve an intolerable emotional state. These acts are not crazy, they are briefly effective and recognizing their meaning may be a step on the road to accurate diagnosis and recovery.

Eating Disorders

Most of us are familiar with the modern presentation of anorexia. Alarmingly thin young women restrict food intake, exercise frantically, swallow pills to cause diarrhea or increase urination, and resist our efforts to get them to eat more. The mortality rate of anorexia sufferers is at least ten percent and many more remain oddly and intensely preoccupied with food. Earlier thinking about anorexia suggested that these girls/women were trying to avoid growing up and striving to maintain the body of a ten-year-old. Or perhaps they were endlessly replaying earlier conflicts over eating with their parents—a kind of "eat your vegetables" scenario turned into a deadly game of revenge. Of course, certain scenarios in our culture encourage anorexia, namely the caricature bodies in haute couture and the anti-female excesses of ballet, gymnastics and running.

What may be at the core of anorexia and of its offshoot, bulimia (overeating followed by induced vomiting, also known as binge and purge), is the discovery that the act of losing weight and the sensations involved in self-starvation may produce an antidepressant effect. Most of the girls and women with anorexia are high-achieving, pleasure-deferring, and perfectionistic and as such they are highly vulnerable to depressive disorders. Starvation seems to trigger an antidepressant chemical response, producing a rare ecstasy together with a sense of personal rapture and superiority.

The fact that all of this is likely due to disordered fluid balance and perhaps a frantic attempt by the starving body to produce extra squirts of serotonin provides a link between depression and anorexia. Unfortunately, the response is short-lived and when it wears off, the pursuit of weight loss must resume to keep the underlying depression at bay. Bulimia is a way of giving in to the enormous hunger, while avoiding the caloric intake.

Instead of reasoning and pleading and threatening the anorectic, it is wiser to recognize that what she is doing makes a certain kind of sense. Anorexia is a particularly focused combination of anxiety and compulsive behavior. It seems to put depression to one side while the sufferer concentrates on a new life goal—perfect thinness—which gives meaning and focus to life, however bizarre and distorted this meaning is. Before anorexia will be abandoned, a better treatment for depression must be offered. Would you give up a sure cure for terrible pain, even if the "cure" was short-term and dangerous, until you had the assurance of something better? The task, then, is to understand the dilemma represented by an eating disorder and provide something better—namely effective medicine and personal support. Forceful and effective treatment for eating disorders can lead to serious ethical dilemmas around the issues of personal autonomy and consent to treatment. The anorectic may prefer to argue her case for being left alone to starve in ecstasy but such an abstract argument may result in death. We are now fairly certain eating disorders are a major mental illness with disordered brain chemistry and seriously distorted judgment. This allows us as parents and therapists to supersede the judgment of the anorectic and carry on with treatment.

Key Points

It is important to remember that many psychiatric disorders may be related:

- anxiety, phobias, and obsessive-compulsive disorder often exist before depression and get worse with depression

- ADHD may be linked to the occurrence of depression

- delinquent behavior is often a result of depression

- a few cases of depression are bipolar and have "ups" (hypomanic states) as well as "downs"

- schizophrenia can mimic clinical depression

- self-mutilation gives some relief to victims of depression or are coping mechanisms for depression

- eating disorders may be preceded by depression or obsessive-compulsive disorder, and may be in combination with them

• 4 •

Anger and Depression

Why Does This Kid Make Me So Mad?

Depressed children often come to a psychiatrist's office because of behavior that is intensely annoying to their parents. One 12-year-old, who answered "I don't know" to almost all questions, had been refusing to do schoolwork for several months. He offered no excuses, had no suggestions, and was unmoved by the increasingly frantic efforts of his parents to help him pass his year. He was fighting quite viciously with a younger brother—really hurting him—and he argued in the most pointless way about all of his mom's decisions. Nothing she did was right, even though he wouldn't propose alternatives. The urge to throttle this boy was pretty strong.

Lara, aged 13 years, would come home after school, slam the door and fling her book bag in the corner. Her mom told her to pick up her things and Lara would scream about how she was always being hassled and how much she hated living in this house.

The intensity of her outbursts caused her parents to keep their distance, especially since Lara said that she just wanted to be left alone. It was quite tempting to leave Lara alone.

Other children will also show an intense irritability during a depressive episode and once the diagnosis is clear, the reasons for their irritability may become clear. As well as being irritable, some depressed kids will begin illegal behavior in a kind of pseudo-delinquent style. Boys will start skipping school, smoke marijuana, and perhaps get involved in fights, theft, and bush parties. Girls will neglect their schoolwork and begin staying out overnight without permission. They will carve their names on their forearms, listen to the bleakest and angriest music available, become sloppy, and become careless about sexual behavior. Previously honest children may start lying. This sub-group of pseudo-delinquent, depressed people doesn't have a lengthy past history of being hard to manage. What on earth is going on?

Self-Hatred and the Love Test

Adults who care about such kids will correctly point out that these behaviors are ultimately self-destructive. This is a pretty useful clue that something has happened to lower self-esteem. Depressed young people, who feel inadequate, bad, and guilt-ridden due to the attack of depressed thoughts and feelings, will begin to live down to their much lower level of personal expectations. Since self-hatred and a feeling of gloom about the future predominate, it's a ready assumption that their parents probably have given up on them or perhaps never loved them anyway. I recall a former A-student who calmly told his distraught mother that suicide wasn't a problem for him and shouldn't be for her either since no one would bother coming to his funeral anyway. He honestly felt that his family would be better off without him. In the perverse reasoning of the depressed, he assumed that since he felt he was a loser, his parents would feel the same way about him.

Such behavior is intensely annoying since no one enjoys living with a grouch who seems arrogantly determined to flout authority. What to do? First, destructive behavior in a formerly well-behaved child is unusual and unacceptable. The behavior should be labeled as deviant while making it clear that the child is still loved. The love test for the depressed goes something like this: "I know you love me when I'm good. I now realize that I'm not much good. Actually, I'm a pretty big disappointment to myself. I'll bet you don't love me either. If I see signs that you hate me, then I'll know for sure that I'm pretty awful."

Once depression has been identified as the disease that is distorting their child's self-concept, parents can take a deep breath and control their mounting anger. They can fight alongside their child on behalf of the real person who has temporarily fallen for a false version of him- or herself. The temptation to throttle a child who is cutting her arms and pretending it's okay is understandable. Depressed people can be very, very annoying. But if we identify the underlying disorder and ally ourselves with the potential for positive in the child, everyone begins to behave better. A warning though—it takes time. We may be treated to tirades about how stupid we are to waste time on them, why don't we admit we hate them, and so on. Depression is never permanent. Don't be fooled. Never give in.

What to Do When They Steal

A very few children steal because they don't care about other people and they simply take what they want: no conscience, no empathy, just personal desire. Most children steal because they feel a gap between how they feel and how they want to feel. The stolen object is supposed to make the hurt better. We know that children who are neglected in the pre-school years will steal in order to feel secure, in order to have what other people seem to have. Of course, stealing candy doesn't replace poor parenting but it might seem to the child to be a justifiable replacement. Depressed children may feel empty and joyless. They might seek to feel better by shoplifting or taking a family member's loose change. The difference between stealing and depression, and stealing due to a lack of conscience and empathy, is that the depressed person has a lot of other symptoms. Their lives have no pleasure, they have low self-esteem, they sleep poorly, and they are irritable. Once the connection between stealing and depression is understood, a parent can help the child restore the missing good feelings in a more constructive way. Confront the child, talk it over calmly, ask about depression, and agree with the child that help must be obtained.

Stealing provokes a response that, for most of us, falls between yelling and a ponderous speech about honesty. Certain points have to be made, but the timing needs to be right. Calm down, decide which parent (or both if they can agree on an approach) will do the job and talk in private. Of course, you love your child. Say so and indicate that the love is not dependent on constant, wonderful behavior. But, stealing is wrong because it hurts other people and it won't fix whatever might be wrong.

Restitution and apologies have to be arranged. None of this is punishment. Consequences work better than punishment. They're hard to do, embarrassing, and they reinforce the right messages. If you suspect that the stealing is due to depression, now is the time to discuss what might be missing from your child's life. What are their aggravations and fears? A visit to a counselor to discuss these issues thoroughly might uncover a previously hidden depression and move the child towards treatment. Most children are damaged when they steal, since they feel guilty, angry, and excluded from the world of honest people. Most want to feel better.

Case History: Clair

Clair is an attractive 13-year-old with a sad face, who became so unhappy about her stealing that she sought help. The school was angry and frustrated by her thievery of notebooks, colored pencils, and other supplies. Her family had delivered dozens of sermons and many appropriate consequences when she stole from her younger brothers. Clair would tearfully deny her thefts and complain bitterly of how she was unfairly accused. When objects were found in her pockets or in her room, she would persist in her claims of innocence, only breaking down when all hope of escape was gone. Then her remorse appeared to be superficial only. Aside from her stealing and her lying about it, she functioned very well. She was popular socially, did well at school and appeared to most people to be quite happy.

Clair's biological mother was a drug user who had met another addict and the resulting pregnancy was enough to scare him off. She turned to the child welfare authorities for help. Three foster families in a row fell in love with Clair, but mom always seemed on the verge of reform and Clair went back with her for brief periods. The fourth foster family adopted Clair at the age of four. By that point, Clair had had ten moves and ten anguished separations from people who loved her. She had spent about eighteen months on and off with her mom whose love was intense but unreliable. Clair's mom ran out of money, had no food in the house, and stayed away for days on end, leaving Clair with casual acquaintances. In other words, she failed utterly to be a reliable care-taker. Clair decided to look after herself, since no one else could be trusted to do the job. When moms and dads said they loved her, they would disappear. Clair's ability to attach herself in a trusting, loving way to an adult was badly damaged. As she grew up in her adoptive family, she stole food and money and seemed puzzled by her own behavior. Clearly she loved her adoptive family, but she always had a fall-back position: "I know you love me, but just in case something happens, I'll stash cookies in my room or take something for myself."

Children like Clair will steal and lie compulsively because of their attach-ment disorder. Then they will feel considerable distress at all the criticism and consequences they receive. These reactions lead to a depressed mood of considerable intensity.

Clair's adoptive family cared for her until she was 16, when she left to be on her own. She had done poorly in high school and she had had a series of intense relationships with boys. She broke up with them when they were unreliable or when her demands drove them away. Her par-ents lost contact with her but did find out that she had been charged with theft and was using drugs.

Laziness

Most teenagers can readily sleep in until noon on Saturdays. Sleeping habits might be irregular and much weekend sleeping-in is to catch up. What can really irritate parents is the forever lounging or resting child; the child who doesn't feel like doing homework or helping with chores. Depression reduces anyone's ability to enjoy life, so perhaps an indolent, lounging child is somewhat depressed. The homework may be left undone because of terrible anxiety about being able to do it. Or perhaps there seems to be no point to anything, so nothing is worth doing. Arguing about the philosophy of nihilism doesn't help. Of course, others in the family will have to take up the slack for the non-productive member and resentment may build.

Again, check to see if other symptoms of depression are present. For instance, a child who is up by 1:00 p.m. on Saturday and avoids work on Saturday afternoons, but then springs into feverish social activity Saturday night, is not likely to be depressed. I worry about the ones who don't even feel like going out with friends. They aren't lazy. They've got the psychological equivalent of a flat tire. To understand is to forgive, so if depression is the problem, an action plan can be created and parents' annoyance can take a more constructive path.

In discussing apparent laziness with a child, remember that a certain amount of resistance to adult authority is a sign of autonomy. Mind you, they still need to do their share so training in domestic chores should start with picking up their toys at age two. If their resistance is not paralleled by a display of energy elsewhere—a vigorous sports life, a busy social life, a part-time job—then resistance might be partly despair. Talk to them about how they can be productive in many areas, but total lack of initiative isn't healthy. I'm always encouraged by feisty kids who argue about their rights to keep their room messy. If, however, there's no sense of humor or a lack of pleasure in their indolence, it may be time to talk about what's missing—how they've changed from being more active and how this might be a health problem. Most depressed children with apparent laziness are also highly anxious. Most sacked-out teens, rising at 11:00 a.m., are looking forward to getting to the fridge, then to the telephone. A void in their lives needs to be explained as a symptom of depression. Give it a name and get them some help.

When Your Daughter Is Promiscuous

Nothing is more poignantly painful than a well-behaved daughter who becomes promiscuous. Depressed boys don't do this much because they lack the energy to take the initiative and they don't feel they could appeal to a girl. Depressed females will still get their share of social chances and a few will seek to escape the pain of depression through sex and "love." The love is likely spelled L-U-S-T, but any tenderness and acceptance comes as a relief if self-hatred and self-doubt are taking over. Sex, of course, feels pretty good and acts as a temporary antidote to depression. Unfortunately, as with stealing or work-avoidance, promiscuity may cause more self-hatred than it eases. If a young woman is behaving "cheaply," then this often expresses her sense of self-worth. Rather than panic and launch into righteous speeches and threats, it might be better to check for depressive symptoms and create a plan for the girl to regain her self-respect. Sex, of course, will always be popular. First-class sex, with first-class people, under the best of circumstances, is what we all would like. The depressed person will settle for much less.

Mothers can discuss promiscuity from a vantage point unavailable to fathers. They can empathize, of course, with the physical delights of sex but, more importantly, they can also empathize with the urgent need to be desired and treated tenderly. Once some common ground has been established, the child can perhaps begin to see how she could have a safer sex life, how she could preserve her reputation, and how her current sexual activities are not good for her. Sex can, should, and will be pleasurable, without being careless. Anger, at her parents and at life in general, may be feeding the sex drive, which doesn't need much encouragement anyway in adolescence. Mothers need to acknowledge the accurate criticisms of their daughters and try to work with them to make things better. Revenge through intercourse may be pretty tempting but it usually puts a stop to interpersonal stability for the daughter. Some personal sharing might be helpful here, but if marriages are to be analyzed, tell your daughter that this will be done with a counselor, not with the kids.

Dad's role here is less direct. Dads represent a dose of reality. They can explain to their daughters how crafty, single-minded, and fickle the male groin is. Adolescents are often amazed at how lively adults' sexual thoughts are. It's a point in common with them. We can also explain how much we want our children to have loving sex lives and not just be walking hormones. If the dad feels his daughter's self-esteem is endangered by her sex life, counseling should be heavily promoted. This wouldn't be counseling to stop sex but counseling to live better, including sex.

Boys are also promiscuous under some circumstances. Depressed boys seldom have enough self-confidence or initiative to seek multiple sexual partners. Promiscuous boys are more likely to be having antisocial difficulties than depressions and, far from losing self-esteem through promiscuity, they may gain it. The youthful Don Juan tends to be immature, non-empathic with others, and generally dishonest.

Gender stereotypes always are flawed by their exceptions. There are some girls who are promiscuous because they are anti-social, immature, non-empathic, and dishonest. Most depressed boys, however, are not sought out as sexual partners because they can't take initiatives.

Truancy and Substance Abuse

Skipping school or drug and alcohol abuse may be due to serious immaturity and the pursuit of pleasure *now*, instead of work now and pleasure later. If, however, the teenager has had a good record and their school skipping, drinking, and drug use appear to be uncharacteristic and self-destructive, then there may be an element of depression involved. Drugs and alcohol act either as escapes or as decorations. The hallucinogens decorate mental life with bizarre sensations and alcohol, pot, and tranquilizers provide a temporary reduction in stress. Avoiding school may be the first step in giving in to anxiety, fear of failure and a need to escape responsibilities that are suddenly too huge. The drugs and alcohol may provide escape from inner misery.

Again, the parents' task is to size up the "real" character of their child. If there has been a qualitative change in behavior, from the positive to the self-destructive, check for depression. Of course, if the child is simply seeking thrills and pleasure and seems pretty happy most of the time, then the problem may be one of poor judgment and immaturity. Asking questions about mood, self-esteem, the capacity to enjoy life, and hope for the future can sometimes reveal a sad participant in a self-destructive, downward spiral.

Any discussion about drugs has to get past denial. Most teenagers will admit to culturally sanctioned experimentation. Past that harmless admission lies evasion and denial. The hypothetical conversation comes in handy here. "I know you say you're not in any trouble with drugs or alcohol, but you might know somebody who is. Why do you think they use this stuff? Since it's so popular, there must be something to it." Most kids won't seriously discuss these issues with parents who use drugs or drink excessively, so if you do, get clean and sober first yourself. Then, your kids might tell you that alcohol is a good tranquilizer and social lubricant; that marijuana moves your troubles far away and helps you find ordinary things hilarious; and that psychedelic drugs make a grubby, boring life turn into four dimensions of weirdness.

Nobody uses drugs and alcohol repeatedly just because of peer pressure. If your son or daughter has a key symptom that is eased by substance abuse then the task is to find out what the symptom means and how to ease it safely. If that's your goal, they might talk to you about it and join you in searching out alternatives to addiction.

Key Points

The behavior of depressed children can make us very angry. Often they appear to be challenging us to still love them. The following should be taken as signs that they need help rather than punishment:

- stealing, lying, laziness, sexual misbehavior, truancy, drug and alcohol abuse may all be signs of an underlying depression

- stealing and lying are often due to low self-esteem and high irritability

- laziness and substance abuse may be signs of a life that has lost its meaning and is searching for artificial pleasure when natural pleasure has been drained away by depression

- sexual misbehavior may be a misguided search for love and acceptance

• 5 •

Suicidal Behavior

The death of a child is the ultimate tragedy for parents, and death by suicide is especially painful. By dying in this manner, the child is saying that no matter how much they were loved, it wasn't enough to sustain their life. This message gives a strong hint of the anger that propels a person towards the decision to die. Of course, for the vast majority of suicidal children, the urge to live takes precedence but the struggle is painful and frightening.

Doctors use a checklist to determine the degree of seriousness of suicidal behavior:

Symptoms or situations indicating an elevated risk of suicide
   Male gender
   Past puberty
   Parents separated
   Using drugs or alcohol
   Depressed
   Lost girlfriend or boyfriend

History of abuse
History of violence in the family
Clear plan of action
Method potentially fatal
Hearing voices ordering suicide
Previous suicidal behavior
Close friend or relative suicide

Parents will often be aware of many of the problems on this list, and if they can discuss the situation in a constructive manner, suicide potential will likely be reduced. Of special concern are the early symptoms of depression that may have led the child to a decision to die. Pre-suicide behavior may include giving away personal possessions and sudden serenity in mood. Such a child has made a suicide decision and feels relieved of his or her problems since death is imminent.

How to Respond to Suicidal Behavior

The arguments about why living is better than dying don't always mean much to a depressed child, but the caring nature of the parents' response is useful. A part of a child's mind might be aware that they are seeking a permanent solution to a set of terrible but temporary problems. It is worth explaining that their death will hurt all of those friends and family members who love them and not just the ones they are currently angry at. Also, they need to know that concrete and specific help will be arranged for problems—problems that many other people have lived through. Reaching out to a child's determination to overcome their pain and anger sometimes strikes a chord. For the very angry and resentful, they need to know that the best revenge is to live well. This argument is especially useful for victims of child abuse who have seen their abusers walk away unpunished. Children need to hear that they have an obligation to try everything to make life better before they give up, and during their efforts to live better they won't be all alone. Clearly the goal of such arguments is to establish that we have heard their cry for help, and they will have allies in making their lives better.

Occasionally a suicide gesture reveals a strong desire to change an unhappy situation in a very immature way. For example, a child who threatens suicide if he can't have expensive sports shoes instead of a regular brand may be practicing emotional blackmail. A review of the background issues and consulting the checklist for suicidal intensity should reveal to what extent the intention is genuine. Unfortunately there is some element of manipulation in most suicidal behavior. Should we get angry and call their bluff? Probably not, since children's judgment is not fully formed and their intensity is potent. A very manipulative child usually has a track record of trying to get his or her own way at whatever cost and using whatever threats will work. Once the parents see that suicidal intent is low, then they can explore with the child how the family can make decisions in a less painful way. The process of re-establishing parental authority is always met initially with resistance, but then the child accepts the new system with its benefits of clear rules and expectations, less arguing, and no violence or guilt.

In summary then, short-term responses require a plea in favor of the reasons to live, an acknowledgement of the child's painful situation, an offer to create a plan to help and a firm but gentle refusal to be manipulated.

Long-term reduction of suicidal behavior is an exercise in improving the health of both family and the larger society in which families live. Looking again at the list *(pages 66 – 67)* of symptoms or situations that increase suicidal risk shows that some factors, such as losing a boyfriend or girlfriend, are very individual, but many others, such as parental separation or alcoholism, are part of our imperfect social fabric. The best plans for creating circumstances where suicide would be less frequent, work back from the more immediate causes. One in particular seems impervious to any form of prevention. How could any program reduce the tendency of young people to fall in love and to then suffer the pangs of rejection? Leaving that one alone, we are left with separation and divorce, substance abuse, child abuse, domestic violence, and clinical depression—no shortage of material for constructive planning.

Case History: Robbie

I met Robbie when he was 12 years old. He was failing in school and he had a bad attitude at home. His favorite phrases were "I don't care" and "Make me." His mom was ready to leave his dad for good since he drank after work every Friday night. She couldn't stand the worry about his driving home drunk. He was an auto-body repairman and she was a government clerk.

Robbie stayed with his dad after she left. Dad's drinking remained limited to Friday nights and he arranged to take taxis home. Mom was unappeased. A year later, Robbie told me that he was intensely angry at both of his parents. He said that his mom was being overly critical of dad. She complained that his fingernails were always dirty and he was low class. She didn't trust his claims to have achieved controlled drinking. Dad refused to become completely sober. He said that "that woman" had no right to try to make him into a snob like herself. He was harming no one and he would continue to spend Friday nights with his co-workers, his brother-in-law, and his cousins down at the garage. He deserved one night a week for himself.

Twice Robbie got drunk on Saturday night, vomited, and tried to show his dad, in a confused way, how awful he felt. He stayed home from school one Friday, drank his dad's bottle of rum, and hanged himself in the basement. His parents will never recover from this pain, although it will ease slightly over the years. Robbie's death stands as an accusation to both of his parents that their adult imperfections ruined his life. I didn't feel that either parent was all that bad. Robbie's own life suggested that he may have begun his own career as an alcoholic and, while he was intoxicated, his sadness overwhelmed and killed him.

What Do Doctors Tell Depressed Teens?

If you are the parent or friend of a depressed teen, what does it matter what a doctor might do? After all, only about one in six depressed teens ever get to see a mental health professional. Furthermore, don't teenagers mistrust adults, and don't they prefer to talk with and get support from one another? These observations are true, up to a point. Doctors, including child and adolescent psychiatrists, have training and experience in dealing with depression. Depression can be described to teens who may be depressed. They will usually agree if the description fits their feeling state. For instance, they may deny feeling suicidal, but agree that life is barely worth living, and that they have no hope for their future. It helps teens to know that other people have suffered a similar condition, that the condition has a name, and that treatment is available. Changing unbearable pain that seems to have no end in sight, to a human condition that hurts terribly but is temporary and treatable, is often the first solid hope depressed people have. They don't like knowing that they have an illness, but at least depression is both well known and treatable.

With respect to the second point—that teens prefer to talk with and get support from other teens—adults shouldn't count themselves out too quickly. Probably no one has a more fundamental and natural relationship with an adolescent than does the parent. Genuine concern won't be out of place. Also, teens don't have the benefit of adults' time perspective. They simply haven't lived long enough to have experienced serious adversity, lived through it, learned from it and emerged stronger and wiser at the end. They have loved and lost, but they may not have loved and lost and loved again. This perspective is invaluable in kindling hope and this is the missing ingredient in depressed teens. When a troubled younger person talks to a more experienced older person, a great deal of help may result.

The process of talking with and listening to a troubled person is dignified by the term psychotherapy when the situation involves a trained therapist but many untrained adults can be helpful to young people. A few generalities about psychotherapy are already known by empathic people and the rest of us can learn them. Begin by listening in an encouraging way. Defer advice, judgments, and criticism. The advice that springs to our lips so readily is likely to be ignored or misconstrued unless the whole story has been spilled out. By then most unhappy human situations are so very complex that simple advice is correctly seen as a failure to understand. Besides, listening allows for ventilation of feelings and this act alone can give relief.

Using comments such as "I see" or "that must have been hard for you" are not tricks to get people to talk more. They are spontaneous messages to show that emotions are being detected and shared, making it safe for the child to continue talking. This is empathy and it is a powerful medium for ending the isolation and depression. The depressed person often feels ridiculous for his or her suffering, since the objective facts of the narrative seldom justify serious dysfunction. To be understood by someone else sends a message that we are not alone. Furthermore, if we are understood by someone else who is not depressed, then there may be a way out. It's like saying "I've been where you are or close enough to recognize the spot. But I'm not there now and such a state of mind needn't be permanent." The listening and the empathy create a possibility of a dialogue where alternative states of mind or activities can be seriously mentioned. These alternatives have to be seen as a goal and not as something that the teenager should be doing instead of being depressed. For example, telling an under-achieving, depressed kid to start going out more, studying more, and "getting a life," would only show him or her what is being missed.

Psychiatrists try to create an alliance with their patients to struggle against the disease. After the listening, the empathy and the beginnings of trust in the listener can come to this alliance or partnership. This needn't take ten visits to a doctor, but might well begin with a chat in the bedroom or in the kitchen. If the depressed person's isolation has been relieved, then help in searching for how to feel better is often welcome, even when the sufferer doesn't yet have much faith in the possibility of ever escaping misery.

Practically speaking, a parent or friend who has come this far might secure an agreement to seek out professional help as one option for the depressed person. Someone who is detached from the child and family and who has training and experience may need to take over issues such as medication and ongoing therapy. These first few phases just described might go a long way towards ending or controlling the depression.

Refusing Treatment

Parents are often painfully aware of their child's depression before the child is prepared to admit it. Adults have much more experience in describing and recognizing emotional ups and downs. Children may not have the words to describe their emotional events and they will react to their feelings rather than reflect on them. After a period of suffering marked by whatever symptoms the child has—tantrums, irritability, social isolation, sudden tears—parents' efforts to understand what has gone wrong will usually pay off with an agreement to seek some kind of help. At this hopeful point, many young people will refuse treatment. They won't go to therapeutic appointments or they won't take their medication. Cooperating with treatment means admitting there is something wrong. This admission is frightening and is particularly difficult for adolescents. They are the young ones, healthy and full of potential. Any flaw is a cause for agonizing appraisal (acne, body weight, hair) and a flaw in brain functioning can seem entirely too much to bear. Besides, parents can always be blamed for life's disappointments.

Treatment refusal is a challenge to any therapist's skills, and parents and therapists need to join forces to allow treatment to begin. In general terms, young people can be told that no one is perfect and everyone has health flaws. People need glasses, inhale asthma medication, take insulin, and so on. Unfortunately, it's now their child's turn to confront a health problem, be brave and honest, and defeat the illness. If one of the parents has already coped successfully with a depression, that could be shared.

Teenagers can be especially wary of using antidepressants. They need a lot of clear information about side effects. They often ask about addiction potential—"Will I need to take it the rest of my life?"—and they worry that they should be able to get over depression on their own. I suggest to them that they will need all their willpower to overcome depression. They will need to expand their ability to deal with stress through exercise, music, and relaxation techniques. They will, however, need to calm the anxious part of their brains so that they can sleep and a return to a balanced view of life through regaining a better mood that will allow their efforts to be more forceful and effective. In answer to concerns about taking the medication for a long time, I suggest that the initial trial of therapy to see if this particular medicine will be effective takes usually two to four weeks. Dosages sometimes need to be increased. Then, once improvement starts, several months of feeling fine should pass before dosages can be cautiously reduced. Some people stay well once their medicine stops and some people have to go back on a maintenance dosage. Parents need to help their child accept that life's difficulties are not always short-term only. Children who can accept that they have a problem, reduce the pain of the problem with treatment, and carry on living a good life, are very wise and strong people.

Dialogues about treatment refusal will likely occur often between parents and children and therapists. It is important to stress the common goals of better health, never giving up, open communication and careful assessment of what works and what doesn't work.

How Can Teachers Help?

Teachers are concerned about their students' mental health issues because most of them are also parents, and because they get to know and care about their students over the course of the school year. Recognizing a child's depression at school can be the first step in alerting parents and beginning treatment.

Symptoms in the classroom will vary, depending on the age of the child and his or her particular personality. Younger children tend to be more emotionally transparent. A child who weeps over minor troubles, or whose face is twisted in rage and frustration repeatedly, may have an underlying problem with low mood, irritability, and poor frustration tolerance. The special challenges of school, with the relentless comparisons children make amongst themselves, will sometimes reveal emotional troubles that remain controlled or hidden at home. Kindergarten and early elementary school teachers can usually note which children are painfully shy, unusually aggressive, or extremely sensitive to criticism. For instance, a little girl who constantly erases her work or tears it up and starts over should the slightest imperfection appear may be struggling with high anxiety. The child might never be able to feel satisfaction at her efforts. If her parents know that an A instead of an A+ meant failure and misery for her, they might visit the family doctor to seek an evaluation about depression. Similarly, a little boy with a short temper, aggression at recess, and no friends might well be trying to cope with a low mood that is increasing his irritability, and reducing his ability to learn social rules.

In the middle years of school, Grades Three to Seven, teachers are reliable in reporting sudden drops in academic performance. Sometimes these periods are explained by self-limited family problems such as heart attacks or parental separation. A formerly cheerful child who becomes sullen, uncooperative, and sad-faced may not be a troublemaker, but may slide quietly into misery, avoiding attention, and feeling that no one notices or cares. At its worst, severe anxiety can produce school avoidance with multiple health anxieties and frequent absenteeism.

Elementary school teachers learn to be tactful and supportive in bringing such observations to the attention of parents. The observations are not presented as criticisms—"Did you not realize that your son is failing math?"—but as a shared concern—"I can't quite figure out why he's sliding, but it has me worried. Do you have any ideas?" Most teachers know how protective parents are of their children, so an alliance with parents is greatly preferred over a confrontation. When parents seem blind to the concerns expressed by a teacher, the matter may need to be discussed with colleagues who could put the child in touch with other professional services available in the educational system. Guidance teachers, psychologists, and social workers may be available to help alert parents to their child's problems.

Added to the burden of being depressed is the sense that schoolwork is sliding towards failure. Depression makes it difficult to concentrate and the condition reduces any sense of achievement associated with a good effort at school. Parents can often help their child with these worries by setting a new perspective. Regaining health comes first, and then it will be time to focus on school.

Parents can approach the school, having discussed the options with their child, and set up a reduced timetable. Doing some school-work at home might be a good way to monitor mood. Even doing a little bit means that the depression isn't winning. Schools don't need to know all the details of the child's problem but a clear letter from a doctor stating that the illness prevents full attendance but allows for some work to proceed can both protect the child's confidentiality and keep the door open for academic recovery.

Parents need to be cautious about how much detail they provide and about how many school people they trust with the information. They need to emphasize that this is a private medical history and is not to be entered on any permanent scholastic record any more than would be a skiing accident.

Homework, that is, schoolwork made available at home, should be offered as an option. It is a delight to someone recovering from depression to realize that they can concentrate enough to read and do mathematics. The goal is not to race and catch up, but to test how well the brain is doing.

• • •

During and after puberty, management of emotional disorders requires an additional appreciation for the growing independence of a young student. At 18, a suicidal student has considerable autonomy and can manage personal decisions about getting help. In between, tact and compromise help bridge the gap between "Don't you dare tell my parents!" and "Thank you so much for telling us." Remember that autonomy and confidentiality must not stand in the way of identifying a problem and its possible solutions, especially if the person's judgment is reduced by both immaturity and a psychiatric problem. With patience, most students can be convinced of the benefit of involving parents and doctors. Students can sometimes be reassured that parents won't be told just yet, providing the student accepts some counseling. Once matters are moving ahead, it is easier for a student to save face with parents by saying that they have acted responsibly by seeking help and they are now in need of including their parents for practical reasons such as paying for a prescription.

When an adolescent continually shares painful information with a trusted teacher about suicidal feelings, problems with addiction, or any situation that is dangerous, there often arises a particularly intense dependency on the teacher. Rather than feeling trusted and privileged and important, the teacher might well identify such a situation as cause for alarm. At this point, the situation will need to be shared with a health care professional. The student is in clear need of treatment. Nothing can be more painful to a teacher than a suicidal student who has extracted a promise that their secret be kept. Teachers are usually helpful and compassionate, but all of us know the feeling of being out of our depth. Any use of emotional blackmail—"If you tell anyone, it will be a betrayal and I might do something awful"—should confirm that a painful combination of depression, anger, and dependency now qualifies such a student for emergency assistance.

Understanding Depression

As with many illnesses that are hard to understand, depression may lead to a lot of false cures. The best known are outbursts of rage, self-medication with escapist or sedating drugs and alcohol, and blaming others for your misery. It's important to understand the pain that pushes people into false cures, but it's also vital to label these activities properly and encourage people to seek less destructive activities. The victim of depression will need endurance, perseverance, and courage to outlast their condition. Having somebody to encourage you and cheer you on is a huge help.

What about the real miseries of life—the troubles that would make anyone sad and that shove many into depression? What about being dumped by your girlfriend? What about having an alcoholic parent or separated and squabbling parents? What about those who have already moved quite far into false cures and find themselves struggling with addictions, crime, and violence? And what about those of us with personal weaknesses, or handicaps such as dyslexia, serious shyness, stuttering, or diabetes?

Families struggle with poverty, unemployment, chronic illness, and many other profound troubles. Since life is unfair, and since depression is a common illness, depression can appear with this background. In answer to the question "Who wouldn't be depressed with all those problems?" consider that the sadness of depression is particularly marked by self-loathing, self-blame, and a feeling that the person's life is worthless. Family members struggling with intense circumstantial problems get very, very tired, and often feel as though they can't keep up the effort, but they know they count for something. They have a clear explanation for their troubled feelings. Depression from altered brain chemistry all too often has no such clear explanation except ruined self-respect and self-confidence.

We know in psychiatry that depression is "over-determined." By that I mean that it's seldom that anyone gets depressed from a single cause. Most depressed people have been ganged up on by many misfortunes. The first order of priority, however, is to get one's mood back on track. Then it may be possible to fix, resolve, or distance oneself from these very real external troubles. Handing over a prescription without covering the preliminaries is not likely to work very well. The re-balancing of brain chemistry back to where things are in equilibrium takes time.

Only in the most intense depressions do people lose the ability to recognize past and present good qualities in their lives. It's extremely difficult to admit a frightening fact such as "I've got a disease, an invisible one, in my mind and it's called depression." If we can add to the message the following, "It's treatable and it will end with my feeling well again, if only I can persevere," then we can build hope.

Is Depression Useful in Some Ways?

A clinical depression is not an effective way of teaching anybody a lesson about life. It is an undeserved biologically driven disorder. Those who look back on their depression are often more tolerant of the nervous habits of others and sometimes people gain a deeper appreciation of life's benefits and pleasures.

There is a form of depression that can regularly do any of us some good. This is a reactive depression, where a series of errors, misjudgments, and misfortunes produce a fairly understandable downturn in mood. These depressions are usually accompanied by a struggle to understand why misfortune has struck. As Pogo (from the comics) used to say, "We have met the enemy, and he is us." Errors in relationships or self-destructive habits can cause serious pain and such pain is best dealt with by self-assessment and necessary change.

Key Points

Depression carries with it the possibility of suicide. Therapists, friends and parents need to point out the requirement to explore all possible resources to defeat the depression. Discussing suicide doesn't plant the idea. Rather, it allows for easier communication about how awful life is during a depression. This needs to be acknowledged so that self-loathing doesn't take over. After all, if you couldn't work or study, were irritable over minor things, and had no useful or enjoyable activities, it might be hard to create a rationale for living. Why live? Because the depression will end and life will be okay again.

In addition to the checklist on pages 66 – 67, the following factors help predict a higher suicide risk:

- Failing at school
- Having a physical disability (even acne)
- Having little social support from friends and family
- Being impulsive by nature
- Having an explosive temper

How doctors can help:

- Psychotherapy is especially important for suicidal teens
- Talking to an adult gives teens the long-term life perspective they lack

How teachers can help:

- Teachers can be an invaluable early warning system for serious mental health problems

- Teachers need tact and diplomacy in alerting parents about concerns
- Teachers need to know when to hand over intense problems to health care professionals

• 6 •

Family Life

It is difficult to live with a depressed person. They are, of course, moody, irritable, tense, and joyless. They are expert at knowing why things won't work and why most plans are pointless. Wet blanket hardly begins to describe their effects. On one level, it is easy and tempting to push away from a depressed person since their presence invites and excites our most negative feelings— anger, despair, and futility. However, most families have had previous experience with depression. Genetic studies predict that the offspring of a depressed mother have a high risk of developing the disorder or one of its related miseries—anxiety, excessive perfectionism, and phobias. Therefore, there is often an unspoken personal history of depression and, moreover, a history of having survived it and coped well with it. This history needs to be explored so that it can be shared with the younger and newer victims of the disorder. This self-disclosure by a parent can be a powerful benefit for the child. They will be confronted by a more mature example of what they have been feeling. The sense of unique isolation that tempts depressed people, through shame and self-punishment, to cut off communication is seriously challenged. Older people have seen bad times come and go, whereas children in the midst of depression have only their sense that it might be a permanent condition. The parents' message then is to hang on, to seek help, and to anticipate relief.

A tougher challenge for parents is to deal with those aspects of family life that may be blocking recovery or even contributing to the child's depression. In some ways, a child's depression might be like the canary in the coal mine. Family troubles can sometimes be the final straw for children. Perhaps their depression can act as a wake-up call to the family, forcing us to take an inventory of our troubles and begin the task of repairing them. This is not to say that a child's depression is the parents' fault. The deep chemistry of a clinical depression is not likely to be caused by parental flaws alone. If parents fight, drink to excess, break up the marriage, or perform any of the usual follies of our species, then their children will certainly be saddened and angered. Sadness, though, is an observation of pain and not the same as depression. It is certainly possible to be deeply saddened by a family's troubles without being clinically depressed. Similarly, it is possible for a child to become depressed in a well-functioning and happy family.

Parents who are concerned about a child's depression will feel an obligation to smooth the way to recovery by reducing the objective problems in the family. This opens the way to options—stop drinking and get well, or preserve the rest of the family by detaching from the alcoholic. Violence, both physical and verbal, can be declared a failure as a coping device. Then the family members can find new and more normal ways to relate, based on cooperation and empathy rather than on the principle of might is right. Family therapy can and should take place when a child's recovery from depression is delayed by these factors.

The pathology represented by a broken marriage is a powerful contributor to a child's sense of sadness and futility. Suicidal behavior is strongly related to coming from a broken home. There are some ways to reduce the pain of separation and divorce. The first and obvious way is to hesitate before taking that step. Just as we expect siblings to get along with each other, so we should expect parents to do so. Romantic love, which both makes and breaks marriages, is a wonderful and dangerous intoxicant but on the morning after, we can wake to a home reduced to rubble. Falling deeply in love usually allows for a relationship that lasts about two years. Then our brain stems or hormones or need for genetic diversity causes us to experience a strong need for novelty and adventure. This is fine during adolescence but a disaster later on. What if it's too late, the marriage is over, and a child of the marriage is depressed? The overarching principle is that the parenting role must continue even though the spousal role is over. Once this is recognized, then the estranged spouses will do their best to ensure the child's regular contact with both parents. The plans of spouses will be discussed, compared, and examined, but only out of hearing of the child.

Children are bonded to parents by a biological and experiential process much different than the bonds of a marriage. When there is a profound incompatibility that prevents a marriage from continuing, the factors need to be shared with the child in a neutral way so that the responsibility for marital failure lies squarely on the shoulders of the parents and not the child. The assessment of responsibility is an honest and useful exercise, very different from blaming. Children benefit from knowing what went wrong, so that they can accept and grieve our imperfections while continuing to receive our care. They may well hate what we have done since it caused them such pain, but at least they can have some grudging admiration for our honesty.

Case History: Allan

Allan, age 12, has been smacking his ten-year-old sister on the back of the head every time he walks past her in the house. When his mom reminds him of his chores—the same ones he's done for years—he gets snarly and even menacing. Mom feels he's acting like a bully. The school calls her at work and the vice-principal informs her that Allan and four friends have been questioned by the police for a lunch money extortion scheme. Allan is being charged with uttering threats.

Allan's parents have been separated for six years. Their separate versions of why the marriage collapsed are hard to reconcile but the father has been married twice before. His current common-law partner and he have quarreled viciously, and Allan has reported that dad is staying with friends until he and his girlfriend have "settled a few problems." When I speak to the dad, he is quite shaken by Allan's legal troubles. He tells me that he has been trying to improve his relationship with his adult children from his first two marriages, and just as his efforts appeared to be paying off, Allan has ruined everything by "screwing up." Dad did a little ranting and raving and his girlfriend and he had a row, and now they've split up.

Dad's narrative of two and now three failed relationships with women, and a series of rifts with his children, begins to make sense as I see him grow angrier at Allan, angrier at his ex-wives, and more self-justifying. He tells me how hard he works (he's a freelance business consultant) and how pathetic and weak his children have turned out. He doesn't mention what he told me at an earlier interview—an eight month period of unemployment and despair, several months where he refused to see Allan and his sister due to his stress (caused, he thought, by their incessant squabbling), and periods of panic when he contemplated how alone he feels when women reject him.

Allan became much less disagreeable and much more astute in his selection of friends after he received treatment for his depression. He had been feeling hopeless about his perceived lack of popularity and about being too skinny. He had decided that he didn't care about anything except making it in a gang: life sucked, so why not grab some thrills and money?

Although Allan recovered completely, his dad continued to be highly critical both of him and his mother's care of him. He launched a custody action in court and put heavy pressure on Allan to come and live with him. The thought of living with dad and his regular angry lectures kept Allan with his mom.

My sense of this situation is that Allan's dad likely had a series of depressive episodes from his late teens onwards. He reacted to each episode with irritability, withdrawal, and blaming others. His good work ethic and excellent intelligence propelled him into successful business ventures, but left him without insight into his emotional confusion.

Depressed Parents

A depressed parent is more likely to have depressed children than most parents. If these depressed adults remain untreated or unenlightened about the effects of their illness and behavior on their children, the consequences will be serious and long-lasting. We might think that by the time we have reached our forties, we would know whether or not we suffer from depression. Not necessarily. Depression is still under-diagnosed, especially in men. Many adults deal with depression by withdrawing from intimate relationships. This causes damage both to the marriage and to parent-child relationship.

As the depressed adult becomes more self-absorbed in their struggle to cope with reduced energy and hope, he or she might well show a lot of irritability when others demand responses, such as, "Daddy, would you play catch with me?" or "Dear, would you make supper tonight? I'll be late at work. I'm swamped." Spouses on the receiving end of angry blasts or chilly withdrawal may rethink their commitment. Children who are criticized and pushed away by a depressed parent will surely suffer pain, lowered self-esteem, and anger at the parent.

My message is clear: if your child is depressed, undiagnosed parental depression might also exist. Untreated, each generation's situation makes the other's worse. Why not rethink adult habits of blaming others, feeling cynical and abused, or coping with stress at home by working more on the job?

As if diagnosing your own depression isn't hard enough, given that you've had years of practice in convincing yourself that it's normal to feel this way, there are further complexities. Depression has "cousins," such as anxiety states, obsessive-compulsive disorders, and phobias. These cousins can co-exist with depression or exist on their own without depression. Genetically, a depressed adult may pass on a vulnerability to a neurochemical flaw that expresses itself in a slightly different way. This means that adults with anxiety states, phobias, or obsessive-compulsive disorders are statistically more likely to have a depressed child than adults who don't have these problems.

It helps to know that an illness has a genetic component. The responsibility becomes that of nature—a random shake of the (loaded) genetic dice. Empathy for both generations and empathy between the generations should result in expanded therapeutic options and a lot less stress and blaming. If we are all in the same boat, then we can work together on our problems, understand each other, and be a better family.

Studies of suicide and suicidal attempts also reveal a tendency in families to deal with depression through self-harm and self-murder. We already know that if a close friend or relative dies by suicide, other members of the circle of friends and family are more likely to try suicide. Genetics don't exactly determine the way people cope with depression, but a genetic loading for depression certainly makes the despair more intense. Parents who are aware of a suicide or a suicidal example in their own family must be very vigilant with a depressed child who not only has had an example of how to avoid life's pain, but who also may have a genetic vulnerability. Such families need to talk openly about the tragedy of suicide and make an agreement to help and to sustain each other so that further losses don't occur. Kids just have to hang on, to "fake it till you make it," and their parents must not ever provide their vulnerable children with an invitation to suicide by example. Remember, suicide is a permanent solution to a temporary problem, and the other family members suffer terribly.

Abusive and Addicted Parents—
When It Really Is Our Fault

Child abuse is not a specific disorder, but rather a form of behavior growing from violent, neglectful, and predatory home environments. Education about ordinary personal human rights can help children at least label what is going wrong so that they can ask for help. Parenting courses that heavily stigmatize abuse—physical, sexual, and psychological—are already popular. We now know that having been a victim of abuse leads most people to view their lives as having only one major choice involving relationships. Will I be a victim or an abuser? Will I have too little or too much power? Such an impoverished set of choices seems to guide children relentlessly into relationships where they repeat abusive situations. We need to tell children and teenagers how to recognize abuse and how to avoid it.

Studies of the factors involved in suicide show that having been abused by a parent contributes significantly to feeling suicidal and completing the act. When the person who is supposed to love you the most, hurts you the most, the pain is terrible.

Long-term studies of abuse victims who are now adults reveal that psychological abuse seems to stay with people the longest. They say things like "I got over the slaps and punches because they only hurt for a little while, but I've never forgotten the names he or she called me." Parents who are kind and supportive help children through their stumbling and fumbling early attempts to walk and talk, tie shoes, read books, skate, tuck in shirts, and make the bed. Parents who neglect these tasks and are critical or mocking corrode the sense of self-respect that every child needs. Children treated kindly at home have a reservoir of self-tolerance, but over-criticized children anticipate failure, quit early, get angry, and feel like losers.

Physical abuse is more severe at the hands of grown men but surveys suggest that women slap, kick, and pull hair as often as men. The lesson being taught to the children is that might is right. When a situation bothers you, you get angry, blame someone, and hurt them. Violence is a very effective way, at first, of scaring children and controlling them. It doesn't even have to happen regularly. The occasional smashed dish or knocked down little girl is enough to remind everyone that the potential is always present, so watch out. Unfortunately, few other methods for solving problems will be taught in a violent family, so as the kids grow up, they use violence on each other and eventually on their friends and finally on their parents. Teenagers whose best-learned, most used problem-solver is violence will be in a lot of trouble. They get discouraged and sometimes depressed and they can and will turn their violence against themselves.

Sexual abuse within the family involves both boys and girls to a nearly equal extent. The girls feel degraded and guilty. They may physically enjoy the sexual arousal, while feeling strange and bad about their secret misery. Being sexually aware well before puberty often causes them to be hyper-sexual as children and then as adolescents. They confuse physical sex with love, and they often feel they must provide sex to get love. Small reminders of the abuse situation may trigger strong memories of the abuse with intense feelings of rage and shame. The accumulation of personal shame, messed up relationships with boyfriends, and the sense of betrayal by their abuser sets up a supremely difficult challenge. Feeling healthy and okay is hard for these girls.

The boys don't do any better. Their suicide rate is higher and many of them have been taught by their abuse experiences to believe that obtaining sex is an urgent imperative. Sex can only be obtained by taking it from a weaker person. Sex is secret and the social transaction for getting it has secret rules. The victim must be selected, groomed, and exploited. How can a boy feel okay about himself if he has been taught this way? The rest of the adolescent world is infatuated with an open and joyous social-sexual dance, but not him. He may feel he is homosexual when he's not. He may have an association between eroticism and children's bodies. He may simply fear being predatory so much that he tries to deny his sexuality. What a mess!

Parents who become aware of the presence of one or more of these forms of abuse in their family need to take a stand to protect their children. The abuse has to stop so that children can feel safe and so that new and better growing conditions prevail. Parents who recover from abuse have to recognize their roles in how they talk to their children. The yelling, the insults, the cruel teasing, the laying of blame—these patterns must stop. Family meetings are one way of establishing new rules of talking and new goals for the family. Violence and threats of violence must stop. The police and many social agencies can help with this. Most community police departments have a youth division, and all communities have a child welfare agency. If you don't know who to call, you can call the child welfare agency (Children's Aid Society) without giving your name. Describe the problem and they will know which agency to call.

And, of course, the family must have clear and acceptable rules about sexual privacy and what is forbidden. A family that has been distorted by sexual abuse has to let kids be kids again.

Bathrooms are private, nudity or partial nudity is out, porno-graphic material is out, and verbal sexual remarks have to go. The family has to set distinct, healthy goals for itself.

All abusive family situations benefit from sharing the history of how things got started so that parents accept responsibility, and so that the children realize that several generations have often been involved. Once the whole story is out in the open, a family can develop a sense of compassion and a determination to make sure the problem stops with them. They will be better than in the past. The alternative is to hide the obvious, repress the truth, and hurt each other more.

. . .

Addiction disorders have long been a widely spread disease, affect-ing more adults than diabetes, psychotic disorders, and depression all put together. Alcoholism remains our most popular disease. Humans have always sought relief from stress through soothing food and drink, and thank heaven there is some solace available. The problems come when the search for relief takes over our lives and shoulders aside other responsibilities towards family, work, and personal health. As we slide into an addiction situation, be it to food, alcohol, cocaine, or similar escapes, we begin to desper-ately cover our tracks in an effort to fool ourselves and others. If we were able to watch what we were doing with clarity and good judgment, we wouldn't do it. Denial is the lubricant for the slip-pery slope.

When the trouble starts—criticism of our behavior by oth-ers, neglect of family, poor job performance, money troubles—someone must be blamed. Spouses, employers, and kids are ready targets. Moments of self-pity, usually hugely dramatic, entice family members into a grotesque effort to comfort the addict, who acts as a psychological "black hole," sucking up the emotions of the family. "Daddy's sick today so don't make noise when you play." "Hello, John. Ken won't be in today. He's got the flu." Family politics become terribly distorted with anger, fear, blaming, and sometimes violence, increasing stress levels regularly. Broken marriages, poverty, incarceration, frequent moves, and general shame mark such families. No wonder their children have more problems than most. Some addicts are using substances to deal with an underlying depression and anxiety state. Better medical remedies are available. A genetic vulnerability undoubtedly exists for many addicts.

In a pluralist society that involves its citizens in free choices, legal sanctions have limited use. Following a policy of legal sanctions has not been helpful in the USA where incarceration rates for drug offenses are extremely high. An illegal act sometimes adds to the pleasurable thrill of indulging. No social policies about addiction disorders will work well if children have parents who indulge unwisely. Bad models that introduce children to the short-term escapism and the seductive dishonesties that surround addictions doom too many children of addicts to repeat the destructive follies of their parents. Relentless education is an effective policy while we continue to strive for appropriate recreational, educational, and vocational policies that make escape via drugs less necessary.

Addiction disorders clarify a vital aspect of our existence in that they are the largest group of illnesses that can be completely stopped by an act of will of the sufferer. Therein lies both the frustration and the hope for all of these families. Once the problem has been laid bare, often by a crisis in one of the children, the family has a clear choice. The addict can stop using so that a new set of circumstances can emerge—circumstances that give everyone a better chance—or the rest of the family can move ahead without the addict.

Separation and Divorce

Preventing separation and divorce should be a highly topical theme now that we have the results of three decades of large-scale social experimentation that allowed ready access to divorce. The initial hope was to free unhappy and mismatched adults from the constraints of contracts that no longer functioned. The results were to be measured in more durable second marriages (they often don't last much better than first efforts), happier adults (who knows?), and families who stayed together out of desire rather than obligation. This search for personal adult fulfillment may well have been overbalanced by causing a fruitless search for pleasure and rejection of responsibility. For decades, psychologist and researcher Judith Wallerstein has charted the difficulties and pains of the children of divorce in California. Confirmed by others, it now appears that her stories of persistent sadness and anger, a hopeless longing that parents will reconcile, and a terrible and chronic weakening of the security of many children, are the legacy of the search for individual happiness.

Economically, one-parent families do worse, psychologically the children receive less nurturance, and all parties are over-represented in mental health statistics. The diversity away from the nuclear family has not created new and better opportunities for human happiness. It is now time to educate ourselves and our children that a stable marriage is an important contribution to child health. I acknowledge the need for abusive and cruel marriages to end, but when the intensity of romantic feelings becomes the guiding principle for adult relationships and decision making, our culture begins to act in highly irresponsible ways. Children want to do better than their parents. Let's educate them to re-establish a more balanced blend of romance and responsibility. We can't shut the door on access to easy separation and divorce when it is necessary, but we should be so appalled at the cost that we hesitate and reach a little deeper into ourselves to maintain marriages.

Key Points

Good parenting can shelter many children from unhappy events. A secure and supportive home where problems are faced and often surmounted creates a wonderful example of skillfully surviving adversities. For those children where there are clear-cut vulnerabilities, which seem almost "hard-wired" into the brain, more specific measures can be taken. Such children are those with a family history of depression, anxiety states, phobias, and obsessive-compulsive personalities. These children need help in rounding off their perfectionism, in developing a sense of humour, and in developing stress-reduction recreations. Families who make an effort to clear away their troubles will make it easier for children to recover from depression and will reduce the likelihood of relapse.

The following factors in family life can contribute to childhood depression:

- Family history of depression, especially if it is untreated
- Abuse
- Addiction
- Separation and divorce

The Road to Recovery

Despite the advances in our understanding of depression and its co-morbidities, treatment remains only partially effective. The available medicines usually put a floor on the low mood or take the edge off the anxieties. They also come with side effects that may require stopping one pill and trying another. The stomach upsets, night-time sweating, agitation, and insomnia are hard to live with, if you're unlucky and get these symptoms.

The prevention of clinical depression may someday be possible through regular monitoring of brain chemistry wherein rapid re-equilibration of a necessary chemical balance can be achieved—a sort of plug-your-head-into-happiness receptacle each morning, take the reading, and administer the appropriate remedies. Of course, such a scenario ignores the evidence that shows how the pressure of unhappy events can create a depression of clinical intensity. Events can, of course, make us happy or sad and sometimes the interactions between sad events and an otherwise well-functioning individual can overcome the capacity to feel pleasure. Depression, then, can come both from within and without.

It is important to remember that chemistry alone doesn't fix depression. That part represents the mechanical detail. There is a more personal and emotional side of the treatment where parents and therapists and friends make a vital difference. It helps to be understood when you're depressed. Advice and criticism usually don't help. It helps to focus anger on what needs to be fixed, instead of blaming the wrong things. Psychotherapy can help to do this, so that the anger is against the disease and not against yourself or the whole world. It helps tremendously if the family pitches in and acts as allies of the depressed person. It also helps if family members begin to fix their own problems, since there may be more than one depressed person in the same family.

How Can You Tell If They Are Getting Better?

Depression doesn't last forever and even without treatment, spontaneous improvement may eventually occur. Treatments are supposed to make improvement happen faster and provide comfort during the bad times.

When improvement begins, the sufferers may not be the first to notice. Others around them may say that they are less irritable and seem to have more energy. Sleep may be less disturbed and insomnia less troubling. The change in mood is harder to verify. One boy told me that he felt just the same but somehow everyone at home and at school was treating him better. Once mood does begin to lift, the end of the day is the first to recover and the morning period is the last holdout for gloom. During this recovery period, there is some danger if energy returns before mood rises, since this might allow the depressed person the will to carry out self-destructive acts.

Informing people about their improvement is quite helpful, even if there are a few zigzags along the road to recovery. The changes show that the condition has not permanently settled in, but is starting to shift and retreat.

Coping with depression is usually a long, hard chore, but depression does end. Then the sensitivity and decency of the sufferer can shine through and life literally begins again.

Resource Guide

Most of us have access to the Internet in our search for up-to-date medical information. This source is vast and as full of variety as all the Yellow Pages in the world put together. The best sites are associated with treatment organizations, hospitals, and professional groups such as the Canadian and American Psychiatric Associations, the American Psychology Association, or the websites of the Toronto Hospital for Sick Children and the Children's Hospital of Eastern Ontario. Websites sponsored by drug companies may be very attractive but drug companies tend to promote their products and may leave out information about other therapies. Similarly, websites promoting cures through vitamins, minerals, diets, or over-the-counter products may be overly enthusiastic about their products and may insist on unproven results. It's "buyer beware" on the Internet, so try to stick to known, high-quality information. [Note: online resources recommended in the following pages were tested at time of publication.]

This guide provides medical material for information purposes only and is not intended to replace the advice of your physician. The information may not always apply to your individual situation. It is not intended to be an exhaustive list.

Attention-Deficit Hyperactivity Disorder (ADHD)

Attention-deficit hyperactivity disorder (ADHD) is the most recent term for a specific developmental disorder of both children and adults that is comprised of deficits in sustained attention, impulse control, and the regulation of situational demands. This disorder has had numerous different labels over the past century, including hyperkinetic reaction of childhood, hyperactivity or hyperactive child syndrome, minimal brain dysfunction, and Attention Deficit Disorder (with or without Hyperactivity).
—British Columbia's Children's Hospital ADHD Fact Sheet

BOOKS

ADHD and Teens: A Parent's Guide to Making It Through the Tough Years. Alexander-Roberts, Colleen. Dallas: Taylor Publishing, 1995.

Beyond Ritalin: Facts About Medication and Other Strategies for Helping Children, Adolescents, and Adults With Attention Deficit Disorders. Garber, Stephen W. New York: Harper Collins, 1997.

Dr. Larry Silver's Advice to Parents on ADHD. Silver, Larry. New York: Times Books, 1999.

Jumpin' Johnny, Get Back to Work! A Child's Guide to ADHD/Hyperactivity. Gordon, Michael. DeWitt, New York: GSI Pubs, 1994.

ONLINE RESOURCES

http://www.aacap.org/publications/factsfam/noattent.htm
(Children Who Can't Pay Attention/ADHD — American Academy of Child and Adolescent)

Bipolar Disorder

Individuals suffering from bipolar disorder alternate between episodes of excitement/mania and major depression.

— Mental Health Disorders Sourcebook

BOOKS

The Bipolar Disorder Survival Guide: What You and Your Family Need to Know. Miklowitz, David J. New York: Guilford, 2002.
Overcoming Depressions, 3rd Ed. Papolos, Dimitri. New York: Harper Collins, 1997.

VIDEOS

Living Well With Bipolar Disorder: A New Look. New York: Guilford, 2001.

ONLINE RESOURCES

http://www.nlm.nih.gov/medlineplus/bipolardisorder.html
(Health Information: a service of the National Library of Medicine)

Depression

Depression is a mental state of depressed mood characterized by feelings of sadness, despair, and discouragement. Depression ranges from normal feelings of "the blues" through dysthymia to major depression. It in many ways resembles the grief and mourning that follow bereavement; there are often feelings of low self-esteem, guilt, and self-reproach, withdrawal from personal

contact, and somatic symptoms such as eating and sleep distur-
bances.

— Dorland's Illustrated Medical Dictionary

BOOKS

Bipolar Disorder: A Guide for Patients and Families. Mondimore,
Francis Mark. Baltimore: Johns Hopkins University Press,
1999.

*Depression Is the Pits But I'm Getting Better: A Guide for
Adolescents.* Garland, E. Jane. Washington: Magination Press,
1997.

Growing Up Sad: Childhood Depression and its Treatment.
Cytryn, Leon. New York: W. W. Norton, 1996.

*Hand Me Down Blues: How to Stop Depression From Spreading
in Families.* Yapko, Michael. New York: Golden Books,
1999.

*Helping Your Child Cope With Depression and Suicidal
Thoughts.* Shamoo, Tonia. San Francisco: Jossey Bass, 1997.

Helping Your Child Overcome Depression: A Guide for Parents.
Kaufman, Miriam. Toronto: Key Porter, 2000.

*How You Can Survive When They're Depressed: Living and
Coping With Depression Fallout.* Sheffield, Anne. New York:
Three Rivers Press, 1999.

*Lonely, Sad and Angry: A Parent's Guide to Depression in
Children.* Ingersoll, Barbara D. New York: Doubleday, 1995.

*Understanding Your Teenager's Depression: Issues, Insights and
Practical Guidance for Parents.* McCoy, Kathleen. New York:
Perigee, 1994.

*When Nothing Matters Anymore: A Survival Guide for Depressed
Teens.* Cobain, Bev. Minneapolis: Free Spirit Pub, 1998.

*When Someone You Love Is Depressed: How to Help Your Loved
One Without Losing Yourself.* Rosen, Laura Epstein. New
York: Simon and Schuster, 1996.

VIDEOS

Why Isn't My Child Happy? Goldstein, Sam. Salt Lake City: Neurology, Learning and Behavior Centre, 1994.

ONLINE RESOURCES

http://www.cmho.org/ (Children's Mental Health—Ontario Association of Children's Mental Health Centre)
http://www.stressdoc.com/teen_depression_series.htm (Teen Depression—The Stress Doc)

Eating Disorders — Anorexia Nervosa and Bulimia

ANOREXIA is a lack or loss of the appetite for food...NERVOSA, a mental disorder occurring predominantly in females, having onset in adolescence, and characterized by refusal to maintain a normal minimal body weight, intense fear of becoming obese that is undiminished by weight loss.

BULIMIA is a mental disorder occurring predominantly in females, with onset in adolescence or early adulthood, characterized by episodes of binge eating that continue until terminated by abdominal pain, sleep, or self-induced vomiting.... It differs from anorexia nervosa...in that there is no extreme weight loss in bulimia.

— Dorland's Illustrated Medical Dictionary

BOOKS

Afraid to Eat: Children and Teens in Weight Crisis. Berg, Frances M. Hettinger, North Dakota: Healthy Weight Publishing Network, 1997.

Anatomy of Anorexia. Levenkron, Steve. New York: W.W.Norton, 2000.

Anorexia Nervosa: A Guide to Recovery. Hall, Lindsey. Carlsbad, California: Gurze Books, 1999.

The Best Little Girl in the World. Levenkron, Steven. New York: Warner, 1978.

Bulimia: A Guide to Recovery. 5th Ed. Hall, Lindsey. Carlsbad, California: Gurze Books, 1999.

Parents' Guide to Childhood Eating Disorders. Herrin, Marcia. New York: Henry Holt, 2002.

What's Real, What's Ideal: Overcoming a Negative Body Image. Davis, Brangien. New York: Rosen Publishing Group, 1998.

ONLINE RESOURCES

http://www.aacap.org/publications/factsfam/eating.htm (Teenagers with Eating Disorders American Academy of Child and Adolescent Psychiatry Fact)

http://www.hopewell.on.ca/ (Hopewell Eating Disorders Support Centre of Ottawa)

Inspirational Material

BOOKS

Chicken Soup for the Kid's Soul: 101 Stories of Courage, Hope and Laughter. Deerfield Beach, Florida: Health Communications, 1998.

Chicken Soup for the Mother's Soul: 101 Stories to Open the Hearts and Rekindle the Spirits of Mothers. Deerfield Beach, Florida: Health Communications, 1997.

Don't Sweat the Small Stuff—And It's All Small Stuff. Carlson, Richard. New York: Hyperion, 1997.

Life Happens: A Teenager's Guide to Friends, Failure, Sexuality, Love, Rejection, Addiction, Peer Pressure, Families, Loss, Depression, Change, and Other Challenges of Living. McCoy, Kathy. New York: Berkley Publishing. Group, 1996.

Otherwise Known as Sheila the Great. Blume, Judy. New York: Bantam Doubleday Dell, 1972.

VIDEOS

Surviving High School. Woodstock, Ontario: Canadian Learning Company, 1995.

ONLINE RESOURCES

http://www.generalpediatrics.com/CommonProbLay.html
(Common Pediatric Health Problems for Patients and Families)

Obsessive-Compulsive Disorder

Obsessive-compulsive disorder is a neurobehavioral disorder in which sufferers are constantly troubled by persistent ideas (obsessions) that make them carry out repetitive, ritualized acts (compulsions).

BOOKS

Brain Lock: Free Yourself from Obsessive-Compulsive Behavior: A Four-Step Self-Treatment Method to Change Your Brain Chemistry. Schwartz, Jeffrey M. New York: Harper Collins, 1996.

Kissing Doorknobs. Hesser, Terry Spencer. New York: Delacorte, 1998.

VIDEOS

Step on a Crack: Obsessive Compulsive Disorder. Woodstock, Ontario: Canadian Learning Company, [n.d.]

ONLINE RESOURCES

http://www.aacap.org/publications/factsfam/ocd.htm (Obsessive Compulsive Disorder in Children and Adolescents—American Academy of Child and Adolescent Psychiatry)

http://www.adaa.org [Look under Anxiety Disorders] (What is Obsessive-Compulsive Disorder? Anxiety Disorders Association of America)

Sexuality

Sex Education

BOOKS

Changing Bodies, Changing Lives: A Book for Teens on Sex and Relationships, 3rd Ed. New York: Random House, 1997.

The Sex Lives of Teenagers: Revealing the Secret World of Adolescent Boys and Girls. Ponton, Lynn E. New York: Penguin, 2000.

The Teenage Guy's Survival Guide. Daltry, Jeremy. Boston: Little, Brown, 1999.

VIDEOS

The Truth About Sex: School Version. Woodstock, Ontario:
  Canadian Learning Co, 1999.

Sex Abuse Prevention

BOOKS

Something Happened and I'm Scared to Tell: A Book for Young
  Victims of Abuse. Kehoe, Patricia. Seattle, Washington:
  Parenting Press, 1989.

Puberty

BOOKS

Changes in You and Me: A Book About Puberty Mostly for Boys.
  Bourgeois, Paulette. Kansas City: Andrews and McMeel,
  1994.
Changes in You and Me: A Book About Puberty Mostly for Girls.
  Bourgeois, Paulette. Kansas City: Andres and McMeel,
  1994.

Sexual Identity

BOOKS

Coping When a Parent Is Gay. Miller, Deborah A. New York:
  Rosen Publishing Group, 1993.
So Your Child Is Gay: A Guide for Canadian Families and
  Friends. Bain, Jerald. Toronto: Harper Collins, 2000.

Suicide

Suicide is the taking of one's own life.

— *Dorland's Illustrated Medical Dictionary*

BOOKS

Night Falls Fast: Understanding Suicide. Jamieson, Kay Redfield. New York: Knopf, 1999.

A Parent's Guide for Suicidal and Depressed Teens: Help for Recognizing If a Child Is in Crisis and What to Do About It. Williams, Kate. Center City, Minnesota: Hazelden Foundation, 1995.

VIDEOS

One Survivor's Message: Don't Kill Yourself. Independent Moving Productions, 1997.

ONLINE RESOURCES

http://www.aacap.org/publications/factsfam/suicide.htm (American Academy of Child and Adolescent Psychiatry fact sheet #10—Teen Suicide)

http://www.metanoia.org/suicide/ (If you are thinking about suicide, read this first—Martha Ainsworth)

About the Author

David Palframan has been a child and family psychiatrist for over 30 years. He pursued his medical studies at the University of Toronto, l'Université de Montréal, and the l'école de medicine de l'Université de Paris in France, and has been a consultant psychiatrist at the University of Ottawa's School of Medicine since 1978.

Dr. Palframan is extensively involved in community psychiatry for the Children's Hospital of Eastern Ontario, and works with the Medical Council of Canada. For many years he has collaborated with the Canadian Medical Protective Association in the teaching of medical ethics and the law at the University of Ottawa's School of Medicine. He continues to collaborate widely with school boards, parent groups, and child welfare organizations.

In his private life, he enjoys sports, classical music and gardening. He and his wife can barely keep up with their seven grandchildren.

For additional copies of

Young Misery

A child and family psychiatrist discusses child and youth depression—how to identify it, and how to cope.

A guide for parents and professionals

by Dr. David Palframan

Contact
Creative International Bound Inc.
at 613-831-7628 (Ottawa)
or 1-800-287-8610 (toll-free in North America)

Or order online at
www.creativebound.com